£4.00

LESBIANS TALK LEFT POLITICS

LESBIANS TALK

Left politics

Kristina Studzinski

Scarlet Press

Acknowledgements

I would first like to thank Scarlet Press for commissioning me to write *Lesbians Talk Left Politics* and for giving me so much support and encouragement. In particular, thanks to Vicky Wilson for many valuable meetings and detailed feedback on the text as it developed.

Lesbians Talk Left Politics would not have been possible without the contributors, and I would like to thank them all for their time and thoughts. I would especially like to thank Sarah Schulman for sending information from the US, Brian Stone for newspaper clippings and Kate Richardson for the article and pamphlets.

I would also like to thank my friends: Lesley, Denny and Susan for all the good times, Susannah and Gareth for ten years of much-valued friendship, Dolores for surplus review copies and nights out, Jutta for advice and the loan of essential books, everybody at The Positive Place, David for tea and indulgence, and my anonymous friend at the Battersea Citizens Advice Centre who worked wonders with Lambeth Council at a time of financial crisis.

Finally, thanks go to ex-lovers, Maggi, for everything, but particularly for encouraging me to write, and to Mary who helped in so many ways.

Published by Scarlet Press, 5 Montague Road, London E8 2HN

Copyright © Kristina Studzinski 1994

British Library Cataloguing-in-Publication Data
A catalogue record for this book is available from the British Library
ISBN 1 85727 012 6

Cover design: Pat Kahn
Typesetting: Kathryn Holliday
Printed in Great Britain

Contents

About the author

Kristina Studzinski was born of Polish-English parents in the
United States, where she lived for six years before her family
brought her to England. She studied Law together with Moral
and Political Philosophy at Oxford University and has been
involved in far Left and lesbian politics. She is now a member
of the Labour Party. She has contributed journalistic work
and fiction to several lesbian and gay publications including
LIP magazine, of which she was a founding editor. She is
a qualified solicitor and currently works as a Law lecturer
in London. She is Company Secretary of the HIV/AIDS charity
The Positive Place.

Contributors

Paul Barnes is Chair of the Conservative Campaign for Homosexual Equality (TORCHE)

Linda Bellos is a lesbian feminist, former Labour Party activist and leader of Lambeth Council

Bea Campbell is a writer and broadcaster who has been active within the women's movement and the Left

Rebecca Flemming is Secretary of the Labour Campaign for Lesbian and Gay Rights (LCLGR)

Teresa Hope came to England in 1975 from Chile and has been active in the feminist, anti-racist and Labour movements

Katrina Howse lives at Greenham Common

Angela Mason is Executive Director of Stonewall

Lisa Power is a journalist, political activist and HIV/AIDS worker

Megan Radclyffe is a journalist

Helen Redwood is the organiser of Militant Labour's Lesbian, Gay and Bisexual Group

Kate Richardson is a member of the Socialist Workers Party (SWP)

Sarah Roelofs is a socialist, feminist, a member of the Labour Party, LCLGR and a former member of the London Labour Party Executive Committee

Sarah Schulman is a New York-based writer and political activist

Chris Smith MP is Labour MP for Islington South and Finsbury

Cherry Smyth is an Irish poet, writer and co-programmer of the Lesbian and Gay Film Festival

Brian Stone is a member of Liberal Democrats for Lesbian and Gay Action (DELGA)

Peter Tatchell is a political activist and writer

Elizabeth Wilson is an academic and writer

Introduction

While the 1970s saw a series of important gains in lesbian and gay politics, many in conjunction with left-wing reforms, the 1980s gave rise to a right-wing political and social backlash from which we have yet to recover. The mood of the 1990s is more difficult to characterise, though it's clear that the political scene has undergone a radical transformation – old rigidities, certainties and orthodoxies are in disarray, while new forms of politics are evolving. The arena of sexual politics has seen a wholesale questioning of previous strategies and allegiances, resulting in the emergence of a host of direct-action groups, the rise of queer politics, and the establishment of an across-the-board professional lobbying group. Where is lesbian and gay politics heading next?

Newspapers, magazines and television programmes from *Vogue* to *Brookside* have in the last year given unprecedented coverage to lesbian lifestyles. 'Are we ready for a lesbian takeover?', asked the *Evening Standard* in April 1993. Paradoxically, this new-found visibility is not a revolution of our own making and our status as media glamour girls can be more than a little bewildering. Lesbians have always suffered from a lack of visibility, and while nobody would claim that media hype will solve all our problems, public interest of a sort is an important development.

Yet many other battles remain to be fought. We still face prejudice in our daily lives, discriminatory laws and practices, and a lack of cultural representation and power. Some of the changes most of us would like to see include:

- a radical transformation in heterosexual attitudes so that lesbian and gay sexualities, identities and lifestyles are respected and accepted on equal terms
- law reform to guarantee equality for lesbians and gay men, including:
  - the repeal of Section 28
  - the decriminalisation of public expressions of homosexuality
  - an equalisation of the age of consent for gay male sex
  - laws prohibiting discrimination in the workplace and in the provision of services such as housing, education and social services
  - changes to partnership law so that lesbians and gays can marry and gain the same taxation advantages as heterosexuals
  - changes to immigration laws so that lesbian and gay couples are treated in the same way as heterosexuals

- custody, visitation, fostering, artificial insemination and adopᵗ rights
- the creation of a new criminal offence prohibiting homophobic statements
- the introduction of a Bill of Rights in the UK guaranteeing the civil rights of lesbians and gay men
- more powerful representation of lesbians and gays in the media, in political institutions and in public positions generally
- sex education in schools which gives parity to lesbian and gay sexuality

Though few would disagree with these goals, deep divisions exist over the means by which they can and should be secured. Is the fight for lesbian equality linked to any other political ideology? Is it a feminist or a socialist issue? How important is legal reform? What are our priorities?

Lesbian politics is the fight towards the equal, visible, vocal presence of lesbians in society. Cherry Smyth

Law reform is more of an issue for gay men. It's only if we look at more political issues such as 'the family' that lesbians are explicitly included. Sarah Roelofs, Labour Campaign for Lesbian and Gay Rights (LCLGR)

The focus on the law, the view that we can make any serious long-term changes in society by chatting up a few Tories and showing them how wonderful we are is a waste of energy. Kate Richardson, Socialist Workers Party (SWP)

Lobbying groups are effective and necessary though I don't think political lobbying is an end in itself. Teresa Hope

It's as though we know, more or less, what we want but not how to get there. Some favour direct action, others cultural activism, others campaigns for legal and constitutional reform either from within or outside political parties. Some think we should embrace all these strategies.

In *Lesbians Talk Left Politics* I want to look at the relevance of Left politics in today's changed political climate. When I started to research and write the book two years ago, I had a basic faith in the resilience of the Left, but during hours of interviews with lesbians and gay men of all political persuasions, this belief was repeatedly called into question, often by people who themselves identify as left-wing. The depth of feeling I encountered ranged from bitter disillusionment, frustration and powerlessness to a degree of optimism. Overall I sensed a profound loss of faith – it was as though a political space was being closed, written off as an embarrassing and naive episode from the past. *Lesbians Talk Left Politics* aims to establish whether there is still a space for Left politics in the fight for lesbian and gay equality, to look at other political possibilities, and to give an overview of our political options as we head towards the millennium.

Lessons from the past

❝ *Because of the work of grass roots national and international lesbian and gay historians, we have found patterns both in our oppression and in our responses. We can begin to analyse what went wrong and what went right. We are able to record the birth of new ways and to watch the dying of old ones. History makes us, at one and the same time, part of a community and alone as we watch the changes come. Having a history will certainly complicate the issues because simplistic positions will seldom do justice to it.* ❞
Joan Nestle, 'A Restricted Country', Sheba Feminist Publishers, 1987

❝ *There was a time in the seventies when we hitched our wagon to a rainbow coalition of the Left and its life in the streets. However, on too many occasions that rainbow coalition let us down.* ❞ 'Pink Paper', 10 January 1993

Links between a movement for sexual reform and what could broadly be described as Left politics first became apparent at the end of the nineteenth century. 1861 had seen the introduction of an Act that changed the maximum penalty for sodomy from capital punishment to life imprisonment, with ten years' imprisonment for 'attempted' sodomy. But in 1885 Section 11 of the Criminal Law Amendment Act (the Labouchère Amendment) extended the scope of the criminal law to cover acts of 'gross indecency' between men – that is, all other forms of sexual activity. This represented a shift in the perception of punishable sex from a specific act outlawed because it was seen as a wicked perversion of procreative intercourse to a category of behaviour in which the nature of the participants rather than the act itself constituted the crime.

The 1885 Act was originally intended to make provision for 'the protection of women and girls', but this was abandoned. In 1921 a Tory MP attempted to bring lesbianism within the criminal law by proposing that parliament extend the Criminal Law Amendment Act of 1885 to cover 'acts of gross indecency between females'. The proposal passed through the House of Commons, but was rejected by the House of Lords. One of the Lords commented:

You are going to tell the whole world that there is such an offence, to bring it to the notice of women who have never heard of it, never thought of it, never dreamed of it. I think that is a very great mischief.
Lord Desart, quoted in Jeffrey Weeks, 'Coming Out', 1977

The House of Commons neglected to take up the proposal again, with the result that lesbian sexual acts have never been directly punishable by the criminal law.

Among the first individuals in Britain to argue for the decriminalisation of sex between men were the early utopian socialist reformers J. A. Symonds, Havelock Ellis and Edward Carpenter. Issues of sexuality were being explored in the new science of psychology and lesbian and gay sexuality was beginning to be perceived as a sickness of the mind or body rather than a sin. The words 'homosexual' and 'lesbian' were coined, giving behaviour previously regarded as a controllable urge the status of an identity.

J. A. Symonds, himself homosexual, believed that men who desired men had women's souls and women who desired women men's souls. He first spoke out in favour of social and legal reform in an essay of 1890 entitled 'A Problem in Modern Ethics'. He also collaborated with Havelock Ellis on the book *Sexual Inversion*, published in 1897. Ellis was not homosexual, although his wife was a lesbian and he had more than an academic interest in challenging ideas of sexual 'normality' since he himself derived sexual pleasure from watching women urinate, a variation he termed 'urolognia' or 'undinism'. Ellis considered homosexuality to be 'inborn and unmodifiable' and argued that it should be treated neither as a disease nor as a crime. He was careful to stress that homosexual men were not effeminate, but caricatured lesbians as masculine and believed that lesbian sexuality aped that of men. This, he thought, explained why the use of dildos among lesbians was so common. At the root of his perceptions lay an inability to accept that female sexuality could be enjoyed independent of men.

The female responds to the stimulation of the male at the right moment just as the tree responds to the stimulation of the warmest days in spring.
Havelock Ellis, 'Studies in the Psychology of Sex', vol. 1, part 2, 1936

Both Symonds' and Ellis' socialism was typical of late nineteenth-century Utopianism in its idealism and progressive humanism. No explanation was offered as to why certain types of sexual behaviour were oppressed, and unlike Marxist socialism, gender stereotypes went unchallenged.

Edward Carpenter, also homosexual, saw the man who experienced 'homogenic love' as an intermediate type between a man and a women – a member of the 'third sex'. Carpenter strongly empathised with the women's movement and insisted that 'women will save us'. He attributed his understanding of women's aims to his experience of oppression as a homosexual and to his identification with the working classes, thus making the links between oppressions of class, sex and sexual orientation that were the foundation of the feminist/lesbian and gay/Left alliances of the 1960s and 1970s. But like Ellis, Carpenter had a negative view of lesbianism, expressing the fear that 'masculine' women would take over the women's movement. His work was influenced by Marxism, though his particular brand of socialism was based more on moralism than on scientific materialism.

In retrospect, Symonds, Ellis and Carpenter may all look like apologists for homosexuality with little concern for lesbians, but in the context of the late nineteenth century their work was pioneering. The theories of homosexuality they espoused all assumed that it was a natural, even positive attribute, and their pleas for tolerance shaped both Left and liberal attitudes in years to come.

Novelist and poet Radclyffe Hall did more to visibilise lesbianism in a positive way. In her novel *The Well of Loneliness*, published in 1928 when she was already well established as a writer, she set out to change people's attitudes. The tragic story of the loves and losses of aristocratic tomboy Stephen Gordon highlighted both the joy and misery of lesbian existence. The book's plea for tolerance, based on the view of homosexuality as innate, owes much to Havelock Ellis, who wrote a preface for the first edition. *The Well of Loneliness* was judged obscene at a much-publicised trial in 1928, the presiding magistrate being of the view that the book did not do enough to stigmatise lesbianism. Ironically, the trial did much to ensure the novel's success and *The Well* enjoyed a high clandestine circulation in many countries. In 1947 it was re-published in Britain without further prosecution.

Wolfenden and the great reforms

The 1950s brought a marked change in public opinion about homosexuality. Many men, some public figures such as Sir John Gielgud, Lord Montagu and Labour MP William Field, had been taken to court for homosexual offences as part of what appeared to be a McCarthyist witchhunt following the defection to the USSR of two British spies, Guy Burgess and Donald Maclean, both known to be homosexual, in 1951. As an indication of the increased scale of prosecution, the number of offences of 'indecency' between males known to the police in 1952 was 1,686, compared to only 299 between 1935 and 1939. Homosexual men were committing suicide and people were genuinely appalled by the police excesses, the general feeling being that though homosexuality might not be morally acceptable, the moral realm was not the business of the law.

The Montagu trial has exposed the complete failure of our so-called 'civilisation' to find any remedy for sexual perversion to replace cruel and barbaric punishment... Society must realise that imprisonment is no cure for abnormality. 'Sunday People', 28 March 1954

The issue of homosexual law reform was first raised in the House of Commons by Conservative MP Sir Robert Boothby and Labour MP Desmond

Donnelly on 3 December 1953. Both called on the Conservative government of the day to set up a Royal Commission to evaluate the law and recommend changes in the light of recent developments in psychiatry and psychology. The Home Secretary responded by informing the House that the matter was under consideration. On 28 April 1954, following more pressure from Boothby and Donnelly and a growing public controversy, it was announced that a Committee, headed by Sir John Wolfenden, was to be set up to examine the issues of homosexuality and prostitution. The Wolfenden Report was published over three years later on 4 September 1957. It recommended the decriminalisation of homosexual acts in private between consenting males over 21. Lesbianism was again ignored. Sex between men in the armed forces and the merchant navy was excepted from the recommendations.

We do not think it is proper for the law to concern itself with what a man does in private unless it can be shown to be so contrary to the public good that the law ought to intervene in its function as guardian of that public good. 'Wolfenden Report', 1957

Actual law reform did not come about in England and Wales until a decade later with the passing of the Sexual Offences Act 1967. In Scotland law reform was not granted until 1980 and in Northern Ireland not until 1982. The delay was due mostly to the magnitude of the changes in attitude such reforms implied, with opposition coming from across the political spectrum. It was by Private Member's Bill, with the much-needed co-operation of the Labour government, that the recommendations at last became law, though the general impulse behind the reforms was the liberal thinking of the time which also gave rise to the movements to abolish hanging and to decriminalise suicide and abortion.

It was just that the climate was right. All those reforms were brought about by single-issue groups who slaved away for years and years. Elizabeth Wilson

The Gay Liberation Front

We don't believe that any existing revolutionary theory has all the answers to the problems facing us. GLF will therefore study and discuss all the relevant critical theories of society and the individual being, to measure against the test of our own and historical experience.
'The Principles of the Gay Liberation Front', 1971

The early 1970s marked a turning point in the development of lesbian and gay politics. Following the decriminalisation of male homosexuality, the understandably timid pressure groups that had existed in the 1950s and 1960s were superseded by a new type of movement which emphasised pride, defiance, identity and activism. Gay liberation was born in the aftermath of the Stonewall riot in New York in June 1969, triggered by a police raid of the Stonewall bar in Greenwich Village. In August the New York Gay Liberation Front was formed, and in November of the following year the London Gay Liberation Front was born at a meeting at the London School of Economics. Though only a small number of lesbians and gay men were actively involved, gay liberation was highly influential on both homosexual and heterosexual attitudes to sexuality.

The politics of GLF, especially in its early days, were somewhat vague, inspired by the revolutionary fervour of the Parisian student revolts of May '68, demonstrations in the US and elsewhere against the Vietnam war and the general 'if it feels good do it' ethos of hippie culture. The name represented a conscious identification with other self-defined revolutionary struggles, particularly that of American blacks, and indeed 'black power' was in many ways the model for gay power. GLF defined itself as a 'revolutionary organisation', pointing out that the taboo against homosexuality was so deeply embedded in western society that only a radical transformation of that society's structures could liberate lesbians and gays. This could not be done by others, but only by lesbians and gays for themselves. So gay liberation was largely about personal liberation and according to those involved at the time was not part of a wider socialist project (American political activist Barbara Gittings has expressed the view that because of its chaotic nature, gay liberation could not be subsumed by the Left). Nevertheless, Marxist ideas of social construction did exert an influence, and gay liberation is often categorised as part of the New Left.

The impulse that drew lesbians and gay men together when GLF was founded arose from our common experience as homosexuals. It wasn't particularly to do with any wider left-wing or socialist ideology. It was a movement for homosexual rights. Angela Mason, Stonewall

The major splits that developed from the middle of 1971, including a rift between the women and men involved, were fatally to affect GLF's cohesiveness. But the politics of gay liberation had begun to spread into wider communities. In 1975 the Gay Labour Group was born and the Communist Party and smaller revolutionary groups were soon to explore the causes of homosexual oppression and to recognise lesbian and gay groups within their own organisations. A number of sub-groups were established in the trades unions, mostly in white-collar public-sector unions such as NALGO (1976). In 1974 the Liberals made a commitment to support an equal age of consent for gay male sex – the first party to do so. And in 1976 a group of gay Conservatives was established.

Feminism and the Left

The 1970s spawned not just gay liberation but women's liberation, a more radical version of earlier, essentially liberal movements for women's rights.

How closely aligned the Women's Liberation Movement (WLM) was to the Left in Britain is a matter for debate. Certainly New Left notions of domination, alienation and repression were influential on feminist politics in general and there were groups who aligned themselves within existing left-wing thinking – for instance, Socialist and Marxist feminists. But there were also sections of the movement such as Radical feminists who placed the fight for women's liberation at the centre of their politics and were more wary of the established Left.

The women's movement, perhaps more than the lesbian and gay liberation movement, was closely identified with the Left. But it wasn't wholly identified and there were many struggles between Socialist feminists and Radical feminists. Angela Mason, Stonewall

The Women's Liberation Movement in Britain was born both of the Left and of a critique of the Left. Bea Campbell

The differences between Radical and Socialist feminists were to do with priorities. Radical feminists saw men's oppression of women as the fundamental power differential governing society, while Socialist feminists believed that sexual politics was secondary to class politics.

Unless revolution uproots the basic, social organisation, the biological family ... the tapeworm of exploitation can never be annihilated. We shall need a sexual revolution much larger than – inclusive of – a socialist one to truly eradicate all class systems.
Shulamith Firestone, 'The Dialetics of Sex', 1970

Radical feminists were wary of participation in established political organisations, which they believed were structured according to male-identified hierarchical principles. They tended to organise as separatists at grass-roots level, campaigning on issues such as male violence and pornography. Socialist feminists saw existing political institutions as important sites of struggle and sought to make feminism compatible with Marxist thinking. Although the distinction between Radical and Socialist feminism was sometimes blurred – Radical feminist theories of language, representation and the construction of knowledge were often adopted by Socialist feminists and Marxist analysis by Radical feminists – differences were so bitterly fought over that by 1980 it had become impossible to organise a national WLM conference.

Lesbians and feminism

In the early days of the WLM many of the lesbians involved chose not to reveal their sexuality, partly out of fear of prejudice from individuals and partly because of the hostility of feminists anxious to defend the women's movement from the charge of lesbianism. But at the Skegness Women's

Liberation Conference of 16-17 October 1971, women from GLF raised the issue of sexuality and overturned the Maoist leadership in its attempts to disown lesbianism as a bourgeois deviation. The first national lesbian conference was held in Canterbury in April 1974 and at the Edinburgh conference later that year, the WLM adopted as its sixth demand: 'The end to all discrimination against lesbians and the right to define our own sexuality.' Even so, there remained a group who insisted that lesbianism was a 'bourgeois aberration' that would disappear with capitalism.

Given this unpromising start, it is perhaps surprising that lesbian politics achieved such significance within the women's movement. Yet by 1970 in the US, 'Woman-Identified Woman' (New England Free Press), a paper published by New York radical lesbians, presented lesbianism as the only feminist choice. Relying on a selective reading of Engels' *Origins of the State, Family and Private Property* (1884), the paper proclaimed a war against men which could be fought only from a lesbian position. In Britain the issue was taken up by a variety of groups including Revolutionary feminists and Radical feminists and was outlined most famously in a paper published in 1979 by the Leeds Revolutionary Feminist Group. Political lesbianism later came to be identified increasingly with Radical feminism and it was suggested that political lesbianism involved outlawing 'politically incorrect' sexual practices such as any form of penetrative sex or objectification.

Men are the enemy. Heterosexual women are collaborators with the enemy. All the good work that our heterosexual feminist sisters do for women is undermined by the counter-revolutionary activity they engage in with men. Being a heterosexual feminist is like being in the resistance in Nazi-occupied Europe where in the daytime you blow up a bridge, in the evening you rush to repair it. Leeds Revolutionary Feminist Group, 'Political Lesbianism: the Case Against Heterosexuality', 1979

Although political lesbianism turned the tables to give lesbians the moral and political high ground, many lesbians felt that it didn't represent their own feelings and beliefs about their sexuality – lesbianism wasn't merely a political strategy to be adopted and discarded at will. Separatism went hand-in-hand with political lesbianism and many lesbian feminists did, for a time, become separatists, though the practical and psychological problems this caused took their toll in the long term.

Women for peace

The Women's Peace Movement came into its own as a separate force within the women's movement at the beginning of the 1980s. Its focus was the camp established at Greenham Common after the 1981 march 'Women for Life on Earth', a protest against the deployment of Cruise missiles. The politics of the Women's Peace Movement was essentially feminist: a belief that the arms' race was part and parcel of male rule of the world. And its practical strategy of separatism and belief that women should seek no part in male power reflected the basic tenets of Radical feminism. Lesbians had a strong presence within the movement, though issues of sexuality were never explicitly addressed, perhaps out of a desire to play down lesbian participation at a time when the media was demonising Greenham women as 'dirty dykes' living in abject squalor.

The Women's Peace Movement was never at one with the established Left, especially the Labour Party which at no time supported unilateral nuclear disarmament. From the point of view of many of the women involved, the established Left was organised on patriarchal principles and ignored the central question of masculinity in its analysis of the arms build-up.

I find the Left oppressive, using women's energy, using women tokenistically. Male political gurus have no meaning to me.
Katrina Howse

The sheer scale and longevity of the Greenham protest, as well as its tactics of non-violent direct action – cutting down fences, street theatre, break-ins and spinning webs around the base – were a source of inspiration to many women. But some feminists criticised the movement's philosophy as essentialist – in that it saw men as inherently violent and women as not – and believed that it perpetuated outmoded anti-feminist stereotypes of women as nurturers, carers and earth-mothers. This ran contrary to a Socialist or Marxist belief that it is social conditions, not nature, that determine gender roles. Others saw the fight for peace as a diversion of women's energy from the struggle for equality.

Feminism in the 1990s

The spirit of 1970s sisterhood collapsed in the 1980s. The strengthening of the Right certainly played its part but wasn't in itself devastating. Most destructive were the conflicts within the movement itself: Radical feminists opposed Socialist feminists; political lesbians denounced heterosexuals and bisexuals; arguments over the extent to which SM sex was acceptable divided the lesbian communities; endless debates about pornography and censorship seemed irreconcilable. And most importantly, working-class women and black women challenged the dominance of the WLM by white middle-class feminists promoting essentially white middle-class agendas.

Feminism was the rallying call for many of us until we realised as white women that it had failed to address the needs of black women.
Cherry Smyth

I think the whole idea of 'sisterhood' had more resonance at the beginning of the movement because so many women were married and at home with children. You could make common cause across classes. Elizabeth Wilson

If feminism is going to change the world as it ought to and, indeed, it must, we are going to have to find a way of negotiating difference. Linda Bellos

Towards the end of the 1980s, the political will and energy behind feminism seemed to have dissipated, begging the question: what is left of the women's movement today?

There are many women's movements. What there isn't now is a Women's Liberation Movement. I think that what we have today are all sorts of diverse networks of women's activism. Bea Campbell

I don't think the feminist movement is dead. We haven't got a single movement because it has become too big but we do have all sorts of different campaigns, very healthy campaigns. Teresa Hope

Recently there have been signs of feminism re-inventing itself. America's 'bad girls' – Naomi Wolf, Katie Roiphe and Camille Paglia – have made significant in-roads in putting feminism on the mainstream agenda and provoking serious debate. Inevitably their work involves a re-evaluation of feminist aims, a new set of priorities and some criticism of where feminism in the 1970s and 1980s went wrong. Naomi Wolf in her book *Fire With Fire* has criticised 1970s feminism for casting women as victims, being too academic, idealising lesbianism and being completely out of touch with present-day concerns.

We internalised the psychology of helplessness on the left. What I'm saying in 'Fire With Fire' is that it's the simplest things that work on a mass level. Feminism has to learn to be accessible. Naomi Wolf, 'Diva', April 1994

There has been much criticism of 'power feminism', caricatured as politics for careerists with shoulder pads or for the girl who wants to be one of the boys. But whatever its faults – for example, its strong anti-lesbian undercurrent – the presence of power feminism is profoundly important as the twenty-first century approaches. The bad girls speak the language of those of us who cannot afford the luxury of retreating into the dead-end, esoteric world feminism has become. Before any feminist movement can progress, the criticisms power feminism makes must be addressed.

The GLC experience

Ken Livingstone's decision in 1981 to commit the Labour-controlled GLC to fighting discrimination against lesbians and gays was the product of changes occurring within a section of the Labour Party at the time. This British 'New Left' – with Tony Benn at its centre – embraced the racial and sexual politics of the American New Left of the late 1960s and questioned the mind-set of traditional Labourism, specifically its emphasis on trades unionism and sole aim of creating a fairer distribution of wealth within the capitalist system. Since the general election of 1979 had returned a Conservative government, ending Labour's five-year reign, one of the New Left's strategies was to use Labour's base in local councils to push through reforms.

The modernisation of Labourism in the late 1970s and certainly in the 1980s meant that the pressure of feminism on the one hand and the quest within some local authorities to identify new constituencies other than a settled white working class on the other sealed a new relationship between ethnic minorities, sexual minorities and physical minorities. People or constituencies who felt hitherto unrepresented were for the first time invited into a new kind of alliance. London was the paradigm for that, but I think it was something that didn't describe a tradition; it was an entirely new conjuncture. And it arose because a settled white working class was no longer a sufficient constituency for Labour in London. It had to create a social base and it saw that new social base among Irish citizens, among black citizens, among gay citizens, among women, among people who needed and were entitled to the resources of the state. Bea Campbell

The GLC implemented a wide range of lesbian and gay initiatives in the areas of employment, housing, law enforcement, the arts and recreation. Other policies were directed towards women, including the establishment of a GLC Women's Committee. By 1984 nearly £300,000 in grants had been allocated to lesbian and gay groups, and £750,000 had been paid out to establish the London Lesbian and Gay Centre. Other London boroughs with Labour councils followed suit and by autumn 1985 at least 10 out of the 32 London boroughs guaranteed equal opportunities for lesbians and gays in employment and housing. Labour councils in Manchester, Southampton and Birmingham were taking similar steps. Not surprisingly, there was tremendous hostility to these policies from Conservative councillors, one of whom went so far as to describe them as 'buggery on the rates'.

Reduction in public expenditure had been a principal objective in the election-winning Tory manifestos of 1979 and 1983, and in an attempt to justify their own cost-cutting, the Tories now depicted Labour councils as fiscal bandits with extravagant and outlandish spending policies. In reality, Labour councils devoted a very small proportion of their budgets to the lesbian and gay communities – Camden spent a mere 0.096 per cent and Haringey 0.06 per cent on lesbian and gay initiatives in 1987-88. Nevertheless, the tabloids waged a campaign lampooning support for lesbian and gay rights as yet another example of 'Red Ken's loony left administration'. But despite the media war, there was a significant amount of support for Livingstone among Londoners, largely thanks to his efforts to reduce fares on London Transport. In the end, the only way the Tories were able to turn the tide was by introducing legislation to abolish the GLC and other Labour-controlled metropolitan councils after the 1983 election.

The GLC and other Labour councils achieved much that was of lasting benefit. The Lesbian and Gay Centre may have come in for criticism, but the idea that such a meeting place could have existed was an impossible dream in pre-GLC days. Funding was also given to projects such as Lesbian and Gay Switchboard, Southall Black Sisters, the Rights of Women lesbian custody project, *Spare Rib* magazine and Silvermoon bookstore. And the GLC did pioneering work in establishing equal opportunities policies and combating homophobia and heterosexism. Most importantly, the council's activities made lesbian and gay rights a publicly supported political issue.

I think the GLC was a good thing in that it created a site of confrontation. The assertion of the duty of a local authority to provide for all its citizens was absolutely right. Sometimes the way it was done was naive, but that was a function of doing something new.
Linda Bellos

The Lesbian and Gay Committee at the GLC provided an excellent model for local authority implementation of lesbian and gay rights. Their material on heterosexism and homophobia helped to legitimate those words and to define the terms for many who employed them at home and in the workplace.
Cherry Smyth

I think that the grants were a wonderful thing because for a lot of people they acted as a recognition that we were worthwhile, that we were part of a general fabric of services. Lisa Power

But not everybody shares the view that 'GLCism' was any kind of salvation for the lesbian and gay communities.

When all these Trotskyist groups got into local government, they had an extremely bureaucratic approach to things. I think they attempted to make an alliance between women's needs and lesbian and gay needs. So if women needed centres because they needed crèches, then lesbians and gays needed centres. I'm not sure in retrospect that what happened in the metropolitan areas was such a wonderful thing. Elizabeth Wilson

In the early 1980s the SWP was different from the rest of the Left because we didn't agree with GLCism. It's a difficult thing to say – obviously we are not saying that the Lesbian and Gay Centre is a bad thing. But we disagreed with the notion that that was the way to fight, that you could just forget about the Tories. We are paying the price tenfold for that mistake.
Kate Richardson, Socialist Workers Party (SWP)

I believe that the activities of Inner-London Labour-controlled boroughs in promoting and politicising overtly anti-governmental gay activities have done a huge amount of damage to the gay cause and have alienated a huge section of moderate and conservative people. Paul Barnes, Conservative Campaign for Homosexual Equality (TORCHE)

In an interview with *Gay Times* in April 1986 (shortly after the GLC had been abolished) Livingstone himself expressed the fear that GLC funding had created an atmosphere of complacency which led to a downturn in activism. He hoped that the disappearance of the GLC would re-politicise the lesbian and gay communities.

Whilst in the short term it'll be traumatic, it'll force people to build up alternative support and campaign in different ways... Abolishing the GLC doesn't mean the ideas and campaigns go away, they just shift to a different area. Ken Livingstone

Clause 28

The abolition of the GLC did not halt the growing movement for lesbian and gay rights. But nor did it satisfy the wrath of an increasingly homophobic Right. The debate shifted instead to a different arena – namely that of education, in particular in London where Labour had control of the Inner London Education Authority (ILEA), which was now to be elected directly for the first time. As part of a smear campaign against ILEA, the right-wing tabloids whipped up hysteria over a book called *Jenny Lives with Eric and Martin* – the story of a five-year-old girl who lives with her father and his male lover – which they claimed was widely used in schools. In fact, the book had never been stocked in schools and was simply recommended for use in individual cases. Labour's gains in both the local and ILEA elections in May 1986 in the shadow of this controversy were considerable achievements.

Right-wing homophobia continued, fuelled by the increasing media attention given to AIDS and links made between the disease and gay lifestyles (the fact that lesbians were a relatively low-risk group was conveniently ignored in a bid to equate all non-heterosexual sexual behaviour with the advent of Sodom and Gomorrah). Minister for Education Kenneth Baker introduced a new clause into the 1986 Education Bill requiring local authorities to ensure that sex education would encourage pupils 'to have due regard to moral considerations and the value of family life'. This was aimed quite simply at discouraging teaching about homosexuality. Shortly afterwards Lord Halsbury introduced a Bill in the House of Lords to 'restrain local authorities from promoting homosexuality as an acceptable family relationship'. After passing through the Lords, the Bill was introduced into the House of Commons in May 1987 by Tory backbencher Jill Knight, but was abandoned after Labour forced a vote on the basis that there were too few MPs to form a quorum. The Bill was to be the prototype for Clause 28.

Lesbian and gay rights was an important issue in the build-up to the 1987 general election. The Tories used Labour's local support of lesbian and gay issues to attack the party as champions of the 'loony Left', while the Alliance expressed ambivalence. Labour's response was to retreat. Shortly after the Greenwich by-election of February 1987, at which the Alliance gained a surprise victory, the party sank to a particular low. Labour leader Neil Kinnock's press secretary, Patricia Hewitt, wrote a letter to a London MP in which she stated, 'the lesbian and gay issue is costing us dear amongst the pensioners'. The letter was leaked to the *Sun*, which used it to launch a vicious attack on the Left's lesbian and gay rights policy. But Labour did not totally renege on its support. When the Election Manifesto appeared in May 1987 there was a vague promise to 'take steps to ensure homosexuals are not discriminated against'.

Soon after Margaret Thatcher secured her third term in office on 11 June 1987 with a substantial majority of 100 MPs came Clause 28. On 8 December Tory backbencher David Wiltshire introduced a revised version of the Halsbury proposals as a late amendment on the final day of the Committee stage of the Local Government Bill. The amendment stated that a local authority should not: 'promote homosexuality or publish material for the promotion of homosexuality, promote the teaching in any maintained school of the acceptability of homosexuality as a pretended family relationship by the publication of such material or otherwise.' Furthermore, councils were forbidden to give 'financial or other assistance' to any person engaged in these activities.

Labour's Bernie Grant was the only MP vehemently to oppose the measure. And to the horror of many lesbians and gays, Labour's front bench spokesman John Cunningham spoke in its favour. In fact, the Labour leadership in general supported Clause 28 on the grounds that lesbians and gays should not be granted 'special privileges'.

The Labour Party's initial support for what became Section 28 of the 1988 Local Government Act provoked fury and left a permanent residue of bitterness among lesbians and gay men.
Sarah Roelofs, 'High Risk Lives', Prism Press, 1991

The reaction of the lesbian and gay communities was immediate. Within days a new single-issue campaign, 'Stop the Clause', was launched nation-wide. The following week saw a mass lobby of parliament and large demonstrations were held in London and Manchester in January and February. Special-interest groups proliferated: the Arts Lobby, trades union groups, Stop The Clause Education Group, and Jews Against The Clause, to name but a few. Most effective in grabbing the media limelight were the lesbians who engaged in direct action, including a group who abseiled into the chamber of the House of Lords, an invasion of the *Six O'Clock News*, and the occupation of a showhouse at the Daily Mail Ideal Home Exhibition. After eight weeks Labour responded to the pressure and publicly stated its opposition to Clause 28. But by then much damage had been done in its relationship with the lesbian and gay communities.

On 24 May 1988, with only three Tories voting against it, Clause 28 was enacted as law and became Section 28 of the Local Government Act 1988. From the outset the wording was thought vague and therefore unworkable in practice, but this did not stop it from having an impact; indeed, there are many who believe the scope for uncertainty about its meaning actually widened the Clause's effect. As early as February 1988 (before the Clause was enacted as law) Woolwich police threatened to close down Greenwich Lesbian and Gay Centre on the grounds that it would be illegally funded under Clause 28. And once the Clause became law, further examples followed – such as the 1993 case of a Conservative councillor who reported Southampton City Council to the police for promoting homosexuality by supporting a film festival at which lesbian and gay films were screened. Clause 28 has undoubtedly had an inhibitive effect on funding initiatives for anything to do with lesbian and gay issues. And most importantly, whatever the wider political motivation behind the Clause, it clearly reinforces the notion that homosexuality and heterosexuality are not equally valid and should be treated according to different criteria.

Changed times

Post-Clause 28, lesbian and gay politics has been dominated by the AIDS crisis. Fears about HIV/AIDS and the links made between the virus and the gay community have led to an increase in homophobia and made politicians even less willing to support us. In recent years individuals on the extreme Right have repeatedly used AIDS as an excuse to call for the recriminalisation of male homosexuality, while Labour has said little. The general mood among lesbians and gay men has been one of disillusionment with mainstream politics, with a renewed surge of independent political activity. Support for the Labour Party, already at a low following Clause 28, has continued to decline.

We have enough rubbish to deal with every day without having people who say they support us and then turn around and slap us in the face – like the Labour Party, for example. Megan Radclyffe

Labour are our hardest history lesson. The last election marked the dwindling of our 'old alliance' with them forged in the seventies. We don't fit into their class politics and are often ('inadvertently') omitted from their version of 'less privileged' minorities. 'Pink Paper', 13 September 1992

But AIDS has not been the only cause for concern. Other abuses of lesbian and gay rights post-Clause 28 have included:
- The conviction of eight gay men in December 1990 for participation in consensual sado-masochistic sex following an investigation code-named Operation Spanner. The prison sentences imposed ranged between two years nine months and four years six months. An appeal against the convictions is now being considered by the European Court of Human Rights.
- The passing of the Human Fertilization and Embryology Act 1990 which makes it harder for lesbians to gain access to artificial insemination.

- The media lynching of the Hackney lesbian headteacher Jane Brown in January 1994 following reports that she had turned down free tickets for pupils to see *Romeo and Juliet* because the play was 'entirely about heterosexual love'. Labour-controlled Hackney Council failed to support her in an apparent bid to distance itself from associations with the 'loony Left'.

The campaign at the beginning of 1994 for the equalisation of the age of consent for gay male sex created a new mood of cautious optimism. The fact that the motion's main promoter was Conservative MP Edwina Currie seemed to signal that public opinion about homosexuality was changing. But hope turned to disappointment and anger when on 21 February 1994 parliament set the limit at 18 rather than 16, again failing to put homosexuality and heterosexuality on an equal footing before the law. The vote was close, with 307 MPs voting against 16 and 280 for (212 Labour MPs, 42 Conservative MPs and all Liberal Democrats voted in favour). Clearly, it was the lack of support from Conservative MPs that caused the motion to fail, but many lesbians and gay men felt furious that as many as 35 Labour MPs voted against 16.

There was widespread anger and disbelief among lesbians and gay men that 35 Labour MPs voted against equality in the Parliamentary vote on the age of consent... if the 35 MPs had abstained rather than voting against 16 the vote would have been carried. 'Pink Paper', 25 February 1994

It is clear that the past decade has seen many changes in attitude within the lesbian and gay communities. Clause 28 and the AIDS crisis have caused many lesbians to unite with gay men, either in pressure groups such as OLGA, ACT-UP, OutRage and Stonewall or in newly formed HIV/AIDS charities. And the emergence of queer politics in the early 1990s crystallised the sentiments of those who had had enough of the tyranny of the feminist and New Left political correctness of the 1980s.

As a result, lesbian concerns seem to have moved further away from feminism or any form of Left politics to become more like those of gay men – matters of sex and lifestyle. More specifically, lesbian political activity these days seems to occur most forcefully in the arena of culture, where lesbian books, magazines, comedy acts, films, fine art and photography are flourishing and reaching wider audiences. In such a climate – post-feminist, post-Clause 28 – has the Left anything special to offer? Perhaps we should be adding 'post-Left'? Post-politics even?

What the Left has to offer

Changes within the Left since the late 1980s have been as dramatic as those within lesbian and gay politics. The collapse of Communism in the former Soviet Union and its Eastern European satellites coupled with a decade and a half of Tory rule in Britain have severely demoralised the Left. Socialism seems to have failed on many levels and no one is sure what its goals or strategies should be. Ideologically, there may still be an argument that lesbian and gay politics belongs with the Left in a common quest for a more egalitarian society, but in practical terms does the Left have anything to offer?

A lost Left?

'The Left' is used here and elsewhere to describe socialist or other radical political tendencies. I see the core of Left politics as socialism, a political concept which can be traced back to Thomas More's *Utopia* (1517) or even to the teachings of early Christianity, though its modern forms date back to the beginning of the Industrial Revolution or more particularly to the French Revolution of 1789, where the term 'left' was used to indicate those who sat on the left of the pre-revolutionary parliament and were opposed to the king and the existing order.

Today socialism can mean many different things – as in utopian, market or Marxist socialism – and numerous strategies are upheld for achieving it, from reform to revolution. I see socialism as characterised essentially by the fight for social justice, the values of equality, community and radical democracy, and the belief that the state has a legitimate role to play in creating a more just society, in contrast to those on the Right who champion individual freedom and the free market. The narrow definition of socialism as 'ownership of the means of production, distribution and exchange by the community' is increasingly being abandoned or downplayed by many individuals and groups on the Left, though a preoccupation with the shortcomings of the capitalist system (an economic system based on the private ownership of property and production for profit) remains a feature of modern forms of socialism.

The increasing lack of certainty about how socialism might work as a straightforward alternative to capitalism is perceived by many as the crux of the crisis in the Left. Some attribute this to the general weakening of the Labour and trades union movements following years of Tory legislation, others to the loss of ideals brought about by the collapse of Communism in the former Soviet Union and Eastern Europe. Others see the crisis of the Left as arising out of its failure to be 'feminised' or fully to take on board anti-racist or Green politics.

As soon as the WLM happened it became obvious to me that there was a crisis in the Left. Bea Campbell

I think there is a crisis in politics in general – a crisis in political thinking, a crisis in political involvement – but it's particularly acute on the Left. Long years of right-wing government and the lack of coherent opposition to that has depoliticised things and shifted them to the Right. Rebecca Flemming, Labour Campaign for Lesbian and Gay Rights (LCLGR)

The Left is in utter disarray and it will continue to be so unless and until the real lessons of the past 50 years are looked at – not just from the point of view of what Lenin said at the Fourth International, but from the objective circumstances of today. Linda Bellos

I think I was once much surer and clearer about what 'the Left' stood for. In the early and mid-1980s it was a broad coalition of the peace movement, women against violence groups, anti-racist alliances, the feminist movement and so on – all represented to some extent by the GLC and by Labour boroughs. There seemed to be a more defined sense of what the goals and methods of the Left were, and it seemed a legitimate and powerful struggle. Although now the struggle is just as necessary, there is a much more fragmented sense of the goals and structure – which is exactly what the Right has worked for. Cherry Smyth

But despite the recent loss of focus, many of us believe that left-wing values are as relevant today as they ever were.

I think that the basic values of the Left are still very much here. It is a question of creating a new and much more innovative strategy. Teresa Hope

I share this belief. There may not be much in the way of an organised Left in the 1990s, but this doesn't mean that the values and traditions of the Left are exhausted. The fight for social justice which characterises Left politics is as necessary today in a world confronting appalling famine, poverty, disease and war as it ever was. In Britain we may not face the extremes of other countries, but 4 million unemployed, growing racism, acute problems of homelessness, chaos in education and dwindling healthcare are more than enough. The Right fails to recognise many of these problems, let alone to offer solutions. Perhaps it's time we revisited Left politics with fresh eyes?

In the extreme

The extreme Left: they're the aggressive ones who verbally attack you on marches if you disagree with their line on how to act as a gay person. Are they the ones who take up the cause of gay rights one week and drop it the next? Cherry Smyth

Lesbian and gay oppression is a product of the capitalist society we live in – liberation cannot be achieved in isolation, the root of oppression has to be removed. Kate Richardson, Socialist Workers Party (SWP)

Militant Labour fights all prejudice and discrimination, including that faced by lesbians, gay men and bisexuals. We see the struggle for lesbian and gay rights as part and parcel of the struggle for a socialist society. Helen Redwood, Militant Labour

The extreme Left (or 'far' or 'hard' Left) generally refers to the most radical individuals and groups on the Left including the Socialist Workers Party (SWP), the Revolutionary Communist Party (RCP) – who despite strenuous efforts on my part were unable to produce a contribution for this project – and Militant Labour. At the heart of most forms of extreme Left politics lies a broad family of theories derived from the work of Karl Marx (1818–1883). The common tenets of the various schools of Marxism are the beliefs that economic matters determine political and cultural life (materialism); that it is necessary to abolish the capitalist system of private property in order to achieve an equal society; and that such a society can only come about as a result of those exploited first developing a revolutionary consciousness and then gaining power for themselves. 'Class politics' is fundamental to orthodox forms of Marxism – the idea that the whole of human history can be analysed in terms of class conflict, the final conflict being that between the proletariat (working class) and the bourgeoisie (ruling class). Marx defined these classes by their relations to the means of production (the ruling class 'owns and controls' the means of production, the working class does not and is forced to sell its labour power to those who do). But do sexual politics and class politics mix?

The origins of the Marxist link between capitalism and sexual oppression can be traced to Frederich Engels' *The Origins of the Family, Private Property and the State*. Here Engels argued:

The first class antagonism that appears in history coincides with the development of the antagonism between man and woman in monogamous marriage, and the first class oppression coincides with that of the female sex by the male.
Engels, 'The Origins of the Family, Private Property and the State', 1884

Engels tried to show that sexual oppression is not an immutable feature of all human societies, but that it arose in response to changes in the way society is organised. He argued that the nuclear family, which perpetuates women's oppression, is the fundamental mainstay of capitalist society. Essentially, the nuclear family is the means by which future generations of workers can most efficiently be fed, clothed, educated and politically subdued, as well as a way for the ruling class to pass on property from generation to generation. Because the nuclear family is so fundamental to capitalism, Engels believed that it would be necessary to do away with capitalism altogether in order to uproot the nuclear family and sexual oppression with it. Though Engels' work has been widely used by both Radical and Socialist feminists, his comments on homosexuality are less helpful. At one point he refers to the expression of same-sex love the expression of 'gross, unnatural vices'.

It is widely believed that the Bolsheviks, who came to power in Russia in 1917, made more significant advances. Their reforms in the area of sexual politics included the legalisation of abortion and contraception and the abolition of an age of consent and all laws against homosexuality. Alexandra Kollontai, a revolutionary feminist who was at different times a member of the Bolshevik and Menshivik parties, was one of the first to produce a Marxist analysis of women's oppression during this period, though her work did not specifically address the sexual oppression of homosexuals.

But recently Russian commentators have argued that the Bolshevik position on sexuality was not as revolutionary as was previously thought. In fact, all laws were repealed by the Bolsheviks in 1917 (making rape and murder 'legal') and although when a new criminal code was introduced in 1922 homosexuality was not recriminalised, an age of consent of 16 was introduced and prostitution was made illegal. It has also been said that despite the fact that homosexuality was legal, homosexuals were still persecuted in the 1920s as homosexuality was perceived by the Soviet regime as a serious mental illness.

A new perspective on the links between capitalism and sexual oppression was introduced by members of the American New Left in the 1950s and 1960s, who explored the humanistic side of Marx's work and expanded the concept of an alienated, disempowered working class to include other groups 'dispossessed' under capitalism such as ethnic minorities and women. Economics was largely ignored in favour of studies of the psychology of oppression and liberation and the critique and analysis of culture. These ideas shaped New Left politics in Britain and were taken up by the Gay Liberation Front. But many members of the far Left rejected New Left politics as romanticism in its move away from materialism and traditional class analysis.

The Left's economic analysis tried to bolt on feminism when that came along. And when black politics and ecology politics came along they bolted them on too. There is no integration. Linda Bellos

A more orthodox Marxist position on lesbian and gay equality was articulated within British far left groups such as the SWP and the British Communist

Party in the early 1970s. This was the result of direct pressure from individual left-wing gay activists and feminists and of the work of Marxist academics who were developing ideas about the social construction of sexuality. One argument advanced was that lesbians and gays are oppressed because they disrupt the supposed universality of the nuclear family.

The way society is organised revolves essentially around the nuclear family. It is an efficient way of doing the various things that capitalism needs to do. Lesbians and gays are completely incompatible with that structure and are, therefore, oppressed. Rebecca Flemming, Labour Campaign for Lesbian and Gay Rights (LCLGR)

We are not born lesbian or gay. Insofar as we are born with anything, it is the capacity for an infinite variety of sexual behaviours. The social construction of heterosexuality is integral to capitalism. Sarah Roelofs, LCLGR

At the opposite end of the spectrum is the far Left view that homosexuality is 'capitalist decadence' which would disappear in a socialist society. This was the belief of the Stalinists who took power in the Soviet Union in 1924, and who went on to reverse the social reforms the Bolsheviks had secured, glorifying the traditional role of women and in 1934 recriminalising male homosexuality. There followed considerable and increased persecution of lesbians and gay men, including the imprisonment of gay men and the incarceration of lesbians in mental hospitals to be treated with aversion therapy. From the mid-1980s there was some liberalisation, with a few Communist papers carrying articles sympathetic to lesbians and gays. It was not until after the collapse of Communism in 1991, however, that male homosexuality was decriminalised (in May 1993) as the result of a new mood of sexual openness rather than any form of left-wing theorising.

Although the view of homosexuality as bourgeois decadence has now largely been discredited, it did dominate within the far Left in the west until the 1970s and was strongly held by many feminists within the early WLM. It is a belief that still persists among some parties and individuals on the far Left, for example in Communist China. Resistance to supporting the struggles for women's and lesbian and gay equality has also been articulated within the far Left on ostensibly strategic grounds with the argument that such issues represent a diversion from the 'real' economic and class struggle. There were many heated battles in the early to mid-1970s before British Marxist groups fully took on board the fight for lesbian and gay equality.

My presence at the Berlin World Youth Festival in 1973 advocating lesbian and gay liberation was subsequently denounced by those who described lesbian and gay liberation as a diversion from the class structure which would create splits and divisions within the working class. Peter Tatchell

Many non-Marxists, of course, believe that homophobia has no connection with the economic foundations of society and has more to do with psychology. According to this viewpoint, lesbian and gay oppression would exist even in a socialist society.

If you say that it is only capitalism that breeds prejudice against gay people, then how do you explain the fact that there was far greater prejudice against gay people in the former Soviet Union than in capitalist UK, capitalist France or Germany? And there's huge prejudice against gay people in China, but there's no capitalism there.
Paul Barnes, Conservative Campaign for Homosexual Equality (TORCHE)

I don't think the critiques of the family that developed on the Left still stand up. You can't say that the bourgeois nuclear family stands and falls with capitalism because it has fallen to bits without it. Elizabeth Wilson

It is very much to the convenience of capitalism that divisions and contradictions are kept alive – for instance, the divide-and-rule mentality that is alive in South Africa. These contradictions weren't created by capitalism but they are perpetuated by capitalism. Teresa Hope

I don't believe that it is capitalism that leads to oppression – the oppression of gender pre-dates capitalism. Marx made the mistake of believing that sexuality and white supremacy are naturally given. But that doesn't invalidate much of the rest of what he says. Linda Bellos

The lack of a clear link between capitalism and sexual oppression is a considerable problem for those who would argue that 'there can be no lesbian and gay liberation without socialism – no socialism without lesbian and gay liberation'. For many lesbians, Marxist arguments seem like empty sloganeering; rhetoric designed to enlist us in the fight for the wider revolutionary cause. What is also becoming increasingly apparent is that capitalist society can be reformed so that lesbians and gays are significantly less oppressed – look at the gains we have won within the existing capitalist framework. The all-or-nothing approach of some far Left groups means that while we wait for the revolution, we lose out on the many benefits that could be secured in the here and now.

In Labour

There is a real crisis of disappointment with the modernisation of the Labour Party. It's a party which is very frightened of politics. It's a very panicky party. It's not a party which sponsors activity, so its response to its own recent history has been to try to purge the daft elements of Leftism within the party. As a consequence, it has purged more or less anything that moves. Bea Campbell

The Labour Party doesn't provide a viable alternative to the Tories. I describe them as 'wannabe Tories', not just because they want to be in government but because of the affluence they'd like as well. Megan Radclyffe

The Labour Party is too conciliatory, too pro-monarchist, too pro-establishment. I think many women, not just dykes, could benefit from the true equality a socialist government could bring, but I don't see a party that has that vision. Cherry Smyth

The British Labour Party grew out of the Labour Representation Committee (LRC) formed in 1900 at the instigation of the Trades Union Congress (TUC) to get representatives from the British industrial working class elected to parliament. The LRC unified existing socialist movements, particularly the Independent Labour Party, middle-class socialists (Fabians) and the trades union movement. It grew immensely in the years before the First World War and its outlook, unlike other workers' parties of the time, was staunchly anti-Marxist. In short, it was, as it is now, a party seeking to change society by means of parliamentary reform. One of the objectives of the LRC was to create a party which would represent working-class opinion through 'men sympathetic with the aims and demands of the Labour movement', though these aims and demands were left undefined.

In 1918 the Labour Party purported to become a more radically socialist party by adopting as Clause IV of its constitution a call for 'the common ownership of production, distribution and exchange'. The 1945 Labour government, which implemented a programme of nationalisation and created the modern Welfare State, began to put this objective into effect. But particularly since 1979 and the triumph of Thatcherite policies, there have been numerous debates within the party over what Labour politics should be about, the most dramatic resulting in the expulsion of Militant tendency in the 1980s. Today the Labour Party appears to have abandoned policies which would give effect to Clause IV and it has weakened its ties with the trades union movement. It advocates more moderate left-wing policies based on ideas of social democracy and market socialism. Some would say Labour has abandoned socialism altogether – and certainly this is true if you believe common ownership to be integral to socialism.

The Labour Party's record in fighting for lesbian and gay equality leaves a lot to be desired. The party did not officially champion any of the law reforms of the 1960s: these were the result of free votes in parliament, though a Labour government did set aside time to allow a Private Member's Bill decriminalising sex between men in private to succeed in 1967. The treatment of Maureen Colquhoun MP in the late 1970s also called into question the strength of Labour support for the lesbian and gay cause. Colquhoun, Labour MP for Northampton, was deselected by her local constituency party in 1977 after she revealed that she was 'gay and proud of it' following widespread rumours about her sexuality.

I am not 'Britain's Lesbian MP'. I am the working member of parliament for Northampton North and I am carrying on with my job. My sexuality is of no more relevance to that work than is the sexuality of heterosexual MPs – something people do not continually question.
Maureen Colquhoun, 'Gay News', October 1977

Colquhoun was convinced that her deselection was entirely a consequence of her sexuality. She expressed disappointment that the national Labour Party hierarchy was not supportive, though she did succeed in getting the decision reversed thanks to the backing of local party activists. She went on to lose her seat at the general election of 1979.

The Labour Campaign for Gay Rights (LCGR) grew out of the Gay Labour Group set up in 1975 and was formally established in the late 1970s as a broad-based group aiming to represent the lesbian and gay cause within the Labour movement (the Labour Party and trades unions). In 1981 it changed its name to the Labour Campaign for Lesbian and Gay Rights (LCLGR) at the instigation of Sarah Roelofs. But despite a growing awareness of lesbian and gay issues within the Labour movement, the party has continually shied away from supporting a policy of full rights for lesbians and gays. In its 'Labour Programme 1982' policy statement, the only proposal is a reduction in the age of consent for gay male sex to 18. This was watered down to a statement in the 1983 Election Manifesto that:

We are concerned that homosexuals are unfairly treated. We will take steps to ensure that they are not unfairly treated – especially in employment and in the definition of privacy contained in the 1967 Act.
'Labour Party Election Manifesto', 1983

Peter Tatchell was the next apparent victim of homophobia in the form of a campaign to prevent him from standing as the Labour candidate in the Bermondsey by-election of February 1983. Tatchell makes it clear, however, that he attributes Labour Party hostility to his candidature more to differences between the right and left of the party than to his sexuality. In particular, he had written a controversial article in December 1981 in *Labour Briefing*, a magazine for party activists, advocating extra-parliamentary protest. This was regarded by Michael Foot, the party leader, as an unacceptable undermining of parliamentary democracy at a time when the party was trying to cultivate a respectable public image.

The reason why I was refused endorsement as a Labour candidate was because of my left-wing politics and not because of my homosexuality. But some people in the Labour Party hierarchy were nervous about the fact that I was gay and that I had made public statements in support of lesbian and gay human rights. Peter Tatchell

The tabloid press mounted a vicious smear campaign in what has been dubbed 'the most homophobic by-election of our times' (*Gay News*, March

1982). Tatchell was vilified not only for being gay, but also for being Australian, an extremist and a Vietnam draft dodger. It is hard to convey the extent of the obscene homophobia that raged in Bermondsey. Local Liberals capitalised on it, as did John O'Grady, the 'real Labour' candidate who stood against Tatchell. Both used dirty tactics, the most farcical of which was probably O'Grady riding a horse-drawn cart through the streets of Bermondsey while singing a ditty about Peter Tatchell. All this contributed to Tatchell's overwhelming defeat by the Liberal candidate Simon Hughes, who turned Labour's 1979 majority of 12,000 into a 10,000 Liberal majority. Shamefully, the Labour Party made no public stand against the homophobia.

There were leading left-wingers who were supportive but they never did anything to express that support publicly or to help me counter-attack the homophobic campaign of the tabloid press and Labour's opponents. I was left feeling isolated and let down. Peter Tatchell

On 10 November 1984 at a rally in Rugby called in protest against a decision by the town's Conservative council to remove a provision from their equal opportunities employment policy forbidding discrimination on grounds of sexual orientation, Labour MP Chris Smith came out publicly as gay – the first MP to do so voluntarily. Smith says he was motivated by several factors: a desire to avoid media persecution, to be honest with his constituents and to be a role model for other gay men and lesbians. Surprisingly, there was little media reaction – a few congratulatory comments in the *New Statesman* and *Observer* and a front-page spread in his local *Islington Gazette*.

The constituency party indicated its wholehearted support and was extremely encouraging and positive. Within the parliamentary party nothing was said officially but a number of colleagues were supportive. On the whole the response was extremely good. Chris Smith MP

Labour's espousal of a fuller commitment to lesbian and gay rights was a direct result of the New Left politics developed by the GLC and other Labour councils and the hard work of LCLGR in the early and mid-1980s. This led to the success of a motion calling for full equality for lesbians and gay men, which was adopted at the Labour Party Conference on 4 October 1985. Included was a recognition that existing policy failed to meet the legitimate demands of lesbians and gay men and recommendations for law reform such as repealing all discriminatory laws, prohibiting discrimination in child custody cases, changing unfair dismissal laws to protect lesbians and gay men and preventing police harassment. There was also a call on all Labour councils to adopt practices to combat discrimination, such as establishing equal opportunities policies, ending discriminatory housing policies and financially supporting phonelines, centres and youth groups. Finally, the National Executive Committee was instructed to organise a campaign of education among Labour Party and trades union members.

Yet despite this comprehensive commitment, there is no escaping the fact that there have been differences of opinion over the lesbian and gay cause within the party. Why was it, for example, that the Labour Party did not immediately oppose Section 28 when a policy in favour of full lesbian and gay equality existed?

I think it reveals some of the problems inside the Parliamentary Labour Party. Part of it is about different opinions and part of it is problems of communication, a lack of awareness of what policy is and a lack of accountability. Rebecca Flemming, LCLGR

It was partly that it happened so quickly – it surfaced for the first time in Committee rather than on the floor of the House. The political antennae of the front bench weren't attuned to it as a lesbian and gay issue. They didn't immediately respond as most lesbians and gays would by saying, 'Oh my god! We can't have this.' I'm not letting them off the hook because they should have opposed it more vigorously at that stage, but having said that, they did put it right fairly rapidly. When it came to the floor of the House they were strongly opposed. Chris Smith MP

Within the many informal factions of the Labour Party, I would cite two main groups – the traditional socialism of the north, in particular in industrial cities and towns, and the more modern, southern socialism predominant in Inner London. While the latter might be supportive of homosexual causes, I doubt the sincerity of the former. The Labour clubs that ban women, the Labour-supporting working men's clubs that maintain a 'traditional' view of the 'proper' family and often have deeply conservative values, are not sympathetic to gay people.
Paul Barnes, Conservative Campaign for Homosexual Equality (TORCHE)

The kindest interpretation from a Labour Party perspective is that lesbian and gay equality was a new issue which required clarification and that Clause 28 was sprung at the eleventh hour. It shouldn't be forgotten that in the end, after eight weeks of intense lobbying by the lesbian and gay communities and individual members of the Labour Party, a three-line whip was mounted which meant that all members had to vote against the Clause. And many leading Labour politicians did speak out publicly against it.

It is crude in its concept, slanderous in its drafting, vicious in its purpose. It is an assault on the civil rights of thought and expression of everyone.
Neil Kinnock, 'Sun', 30 January 1988

There will never again be any suggestion of the Labour Party backing off from its support for lesbian and gay rights.
Jo Richardson MP, 'Gay Times', November 1988

At the annual conference in 1988 the party updated its policy on lesbian and gay rights to include a commitment to repealing Section 28, which is the policy it took into the 1992 general election. There was some controversy when the policy statement was abbreviated for the purposes of the 1992 Election Manifesto, but this did not represent the 'wimping out' over lesbian and gay rights some have claimed. The shortened statement that appeared in the manifesto was essentially the same as the motion adopted by the conference, though it did not include a commitment to 'full equality for lesbians and gay men' or a call on Labour local authorities to consider the rights of lesbians and gay men in the provision of services.

We will offer everyone a fair chance. Stronger sex and race discrimination laws will ensure that organisations awarded government contracts take positive steps to promote equal treatment. We will introduce a new law dealing with discrimination on grounds of sexuality, repeal the unjust Clause 28 and allow a free vote in the House of Commons on the age of consent. 'Labour Party Election Manifesto', 1992

In the recent battle over the age of consent, the vast majority of Labour MPs voted for 16. But why did 35 Labour MPs oppose equality? Once again many lesbians and gay men feel let down.

I can't believe the well-known names who actively voted against 16 – Stuart Bell, Joe Ashton, Dale Campbell-Savours, Bob Cryer, Stan Orme and Denzil Davies. It seems bigotry runs deep, particularly in some Labour constituencies. David Bridle, 'Pink Paper', 25 February 1994

On issues of equal rights for women and black people the parliamentary Labour Party never settle for a free vote – MPs are whipped to support equality. Why wasn't there a three line whip on this issue? Peter Tatchell, 'Labour Briefing', April 1994

If you look at the 35 Labour MPs who voted against 16, virtually all of them are of an older generation. Rather than a left/right split or a workerist/moderniser split, I think it's more to do with the generation of Labour politics they grew up in. The thing that mattered was the class struggle and Labour was in power to stand up for working-class people and poor people. It was an economic debate. Chris Smith MP

The LCLGR, which unlike the Liberal Democrat lesbian and gay group (DELGA) is not officially recognised or consulted by the Labour Party, continues to campaign for lesbian and gay equality.

LCLGR believes we can only win our liberation in a just society, free from prejudice and discrimination – a socialist society; and that our liberation is a necessary part of achieving socialism. LCLGR leaflet

Besides working to gain a full commitment to lesbian and gay equality, LCLGR has won much Labour and trades union backing for the campaign against Section 28, the promotion of artificial insemination, parenting and fostering rights for lesbians and gays, anti-racist campaigns and issues to do with HIV/AIDS. It recognises that the demands of lesbians, black people and people with disabilities often come last and so campaigns to ensure proper representation of all these groups. LCLGR's objectives go beyond legal and political reforms to challenge ideology, in particular around the family.

As for the future of the Labour Party, I think there is as much promise for Labour politics as there ever was. Indeed, given the criticisms that have always been levelled at the party, the idea of a current crisis could be seen as something of a myth. Labour is and always has been a political party of moderate aims: namely, better to represent the interests of the working class. To date this has to a large extent been interpreted as the interests of working-class men rather than women or lesbians. But the party remains in principle the party of the underdog and, not to be forgotten, of the poor. We need to make the Labour Party realise that it is our party too – we are part of the wider fight for social justice and equality. And I believe the message is getting across.

We have made great strides both on a policy level and in terms of raising Labour consciousness. It's now accepted in virtually all sections of the Labour movement except for the most left-over dinosaur types that lesbian and gay rights, together with women's rights and black rights, are very much a part of the Labour Party perspective.
Sarah Roelofs, LCLGR

For many Labour MPs and officials there is still a degree of embarrassment and discomfort about advocating homosexual human rights. This is partly due to personal anxieties and phobias and partly due to the fear that lesbian and gay rights is an electorally damaging policy. Peter Tatchell

One of the things that a newer generation of Labour members now recognises is that while class and economic issues are still very important, there are also issues of race, gender and sexuality, of equality and justice in other ways which are important too. Chris Smith MP

In the trades unions

The 1980s saw a growing commitment to lesbian and gay rights within the trades unions – again largely as a result of the New Left politics developed within Labour councils. On 6 September 1985 a motion was passed at the TUC which called on all affiliated trades unions to:

- campaign for legislation to protect lesbians and gay men against all forms of discrimination in all areas of life
- include lesbians and gay men in all negotiated equal opportunities clauses and agreements
- raise awareness of the issues within their own organisation
- examine terms and conditions of employment such as pensions, bereavement leave and caring for children and dependants to ensure that no discrimination exists on the grounds of sexual orientation

- support openly members who are victimised as a result of their sexuality

Many unions have acted on this motion. In a 1991 survey carried out by the Labour Research Department, it was found that 25 unions representing 65 per cent of total TUC-affiliated membership had begun to take initiatives such as ensuring that partners of lesbians and gays have the same entitlement to fringe benefits as heterosexuals, recommending action to stop harassment at work, developing equal opportunities policies and forming special lesbian and gay groups. One recent breakthrough has been in the civil service, where homosexuality was until recently considered a 'security risk'. After years of campaigning by gay groups, an announcement was made in 1991 by John Major that, 'in future there should be no posts involving access to highly classified information for which homosexuality represents an automatic bar to security clearance.' I know of one instance where, because of the change in policy, a lesbian in a fairly high-ranking position was able to come out during the vetting process without fear of reprisal. The next step, of course, was for the civil service to vet her girlfriend and ex-girlfriends! All these changes are to be applauded, as anyone who has suffered the strain of being closeted at work or has been sacked because of their sexuality can tell you.

Other more symbolic instances of trades union alliance with the lesbian and gay cause occurred during and after the miners' strike of 1984-85. A lesbian and gay support group was set up which made lesbian and gay issues visible perhaps for the first time within some of the more traditional mining communities. As a result, the 1985 Gay Pride march was led by a delegation of miners with a pit banner and band.

The policies many unions have adopted and the rights they have won are telling examples of what can be achieved through equal opportunities. As well as directly improving the lives of lesbians and gay men, the trades unions have played a valuable role in educating heterosexuals about our existence and how we should be treated.

Today the far Left, Labour Party and trades union movement all have a strong commitment to fighting for lesbian and gay equality. But this does not mean that the Left has a monopoly on representing the lesbian and gay cause. Perhaps liberal politics has as much to offer? And are the Conservatives really our arch enemies?

Lesbian and gay politics outside the Left

> 6 *John Major's meeting with Sir Ian McKellen was a positive sign that the government is prepared to consider seriously the issue of homosexual equality, a cause that for so long has been hijacked by the Left.* 9
> Conservative Campaign for Homosexual Equality (TORCHE) leaflet

> 6 *As a Liberal, I wouldn't identify civil liberties, including those of lesbians and gay men, as a socialist issue. One of the reasons why I am a Liberal is because it is the Liberal Party which has consistently been the supporter of lesbian and gay rights.* 9
> Brian Stone, Liberal Democrats for Lesbian and Gay Action (DELGA)

Little time has been given to the idea that there is a connection between right-wing and lesbian and gay politics. The prevailing view among lesbian and gay activists and the media is that the Right stands for everything lesbians and gays should be against, including the legitimation of homophobia and the oppression of women. As for the Liberal position, who knows? This chapter aims to put aside all preconceptions to explore the theory and practice of the Right and the Liberal camps in relation to lesbians and gays. Is there a space for lesbian and gay politics outside the Left? And if so, is it a more or a less hospitable space?

Turkeys voting for Christmas?

It is clear that a gay voting Conservative is like a turkey voting for Christmas.
'Capital Gay', 5 June 1987

The idea of a Tory lesbian seems to many to be a contradiction in terms. And despite much searching, I failed to find a lesbian who voted Tory and was prepared to be interviewed for this project, even anonymously. But there is a thriving gay activist group within the Conservative Party (TORCHE) and I have been told that there are a number of lesbian Tory Party activists.

Lesbian and gay distrust of the Conservative Party has solid foundations.

Although there has never been an official Conservative line on the lesbian and gay cause, from the 1980s onwards the Conservatives have openly attacked lesbian and gay rights, the introduction of Section 28 being only one instance among many. Other setbacks instigated by the Conservative government include:

- the Human Fertilization and Embryology Act 1990, which established a licensing agency to regulate who should receive infertility treatment, including insemination. The Act requires that infertility clinics consider the child's need for a father when deciding whether or not a woman is a suitable candidate for treatment
- the Child Support Act, which became law in April 1993. The Act gives social security officials the power to demand that a lesbian mother gives the name, address, national insurance number and work address of her sperm donor

And leading Tories have repeatedly made blatantly homophobic statements justified by the belief that lesbian and gay lifestyles are 'evil', 'unnatural' or 'perverted'. For many of us, Conservatism stands for bigotry in the name of family values and religion. Gay Tory apologists can only try to excuse such excesses as strategies for undermining the credibility of the 'loony Left'.

Those bunch of queers that legalise filth in homosexuality have a lot to answer for and I hope they are proud of what they have done... As a cure I would put 90 per cent of queers in the ruddy gas chamber. Bill Brownhill, Conservative leader of South Staffordshire, 'Capital Gay', 9 January 1987

In male homosexuality – homos in Greek meaning 'the same' and homo in Latin meaning 'man' – there is a perversion of the human function. It is using the excretory anus and rectum with a reproductive organ... anyone who comprehends the deep libidinal and psychological origins of male and female homosexuality should understand that it is a major perversion. Nicholas Fairburn, Conservative MP, 9 March 1987

What we should be saying is: 'Look, I'm afraid this sort of behaviour is totally unacceptable. You're putting your nation at risk by your behaviour. We're not going to have this in the future.' And that's why we're legislating to make this a crime once again. Geoffrey Dickens, Conservative MP, 'The Heart of the Matter', BBC, March 1987

The 'back to basics' drive initiated in October 1993 tried to re-emphasise the Tory Party's support for traditional family values. This time around it was single mothers who were the most prominent target, though as several scandals involving MPs Lord Caithness (adultery), Tim Yeo (fathering a 'love child'), David Ashby (sharing a bed with a male 'friend' while on holiday), Stephen Milligan (death by auto-erotic asphyxiation) and Michael Brown (having a relationship with a 20-year-old man) showed, back to basics could be used to denounce any behaviour outside monogamous marriage.

Like left-wing ideology, however, Conservative ideology is not a seamless whole, and the party is far from united in its anti-lesbian and gay sentiments. Several individual Tory MPs have taken a public stand in favour of gay rights, including Desmond Donnelly MP, former MP Matthew Parris and most recently Edwina Currie, Jerry Hayes and Harold Elletson. Some people would even say that there is no Conservative ideology at all, ideology being an invention of the Left and Conservatives being essentially pragmatic creatures. Yet it is clear that modern Conservatism is characterised by certain values: a belief in the importance of traditional social units (in particular the nuclear family), a belief in free-market principles, a pessimism about human nature, a belief that rule by an elite is both inevitable and desirable, and a preference for gradual change. But as with all political ideologies, there are many strands and variations; indeed, the confusion over back to basics reflects a tension between support for traditional family values and the belief that an individual's private life should not be a matter for political comment.

I have it thrown at me, 'How can you be gay and be a member of the Conservative Party?' I have no worries on that at all. I think that the Tory Party has within its philosophy a lot to offer gay people. The philosophy is of equality of opportunity, the individual promoting him or herself and getting the best out of life that he or she can. Take away all the barriers that will prevent him or her from doing that, take away the dead hand of the state, allow people freedom to make their own decisions and for a gay person that is great. Paul Barnes, TORCHE

The Right celebrates freedom of choice and it also celebrates tradition and the family. There are loads of ways in which the Right will be permissive because of its commitment to individual choice. Other things will work against that. The Right is full of contradictions and it can live with them quite happily.
Bea Campbell

Libertarianism, once something of a fringe political theory, has become increasingly influential. The libertarian belief in a minimal role for the state in all aspects of life has led to the privatisation of the NHS and the prison service and to the introduction of the 'contract culture' in nationalised industries and services from British Telecom and British Airways to public-service provision. Libertarians believe that it is not the business of the state to interfere in private behaviour, be it in commerce, sexual orientation, the use of pornography or the taking of drugs. One recent expression of this strand of right-wing thinking occurred around the Operation Spanner campaign, where Conservative libertarians argued vociferously for SM not to be criminalised. Of course, in opposition to such views there is also a strong contingent that is pro-censorship, anti-SM and anti-lesbian and gay equality in the name of promoting family values.

The appointment of John Major as Prime Minister in December 1990 following the forced resignation of Margaret Thatcher led to a mood of optimism among gay Conservatives, partly because Major's espousal of a classless society and a Conservative Party 'open to everyone' seemed to signal a new liberalism. This optimism was fuelled by a much-publicised meeting between Major and Stonewall Group representative Sir Ian McKellen on 24 September 1991, which was billed as a preliminary bid to put lesbian and gay rights on the Conservative political agenda. The formation of the Conservative Parliamentary Group for Homosexual Legal Reform followed shortly afterwards, together with a number of reforms including:

- the ruling out of homosexuality as a security risk in the civil service (1991)
- a promise to decriminalise homosexuality in the armed forces and merchant navy made in 1991 and passing through parliament as an amendment to the Criminal Justice and Public Order Bill at the time of writing
- the decriminalisation of homosexuality on the Isle of Man (July 1992)
- government guidelines for local authorities on lesbian and gay couples and joint tenancies (May 1993)

In addition, several leading Tories, most famously Edwina Currie but also Michael Brown and Sir John Wheeler (who are members of the parliamentary group), have taken an openly pro-gay stance.

TORCHE was formed in February 1992 as a replacement for the largely defunct Conservative Group for Homosexual Equality. Major sent it a warm letter of personal support. TORCHE (which is not officially recognised within the party) has two aims: to bring about full legal equality for gay people and to provide a platform for gay Conservatives within both the party and the gay community. Its detailed policy document includes commitments to equalising the age of consent for gay men, allowing gays to serve in the armed forces, equal penalties for sex offences in public, reform of the Sexual Offences Act 1967 to decriminalise consenting acts between gay men in 'public' places, an anti-censorship stance, the repeal of Section 28, sex education about homosexuality in schools, allowing lesbians and gays to foster and adopt, extending domestic partnership law to lesbian and gay couples, equalising immigration laws and prohibiting insurance companies from refusing to insure gay men on grounds of their sexuality alone. In many ways TORCHE's position is radical, although there are some notable omissions such as employment protection and anti-discrimination laws. TORCHE stresses that the fight is for 'legal equality' and draws the line at 'positive discrimination'.

The Tory view policy-wise is that they have no view, whereas the view of TORCHE is very simple: it is just equality, nothing more than that, so it doesn't believe in positive discrimination. Paul Barnes, TORCHE

The free vote in parliament on 21 February 1994 on an equal age of consent for gay male sex was a direct result of the changes occurring within the party. Edwina Currie spear-headed the campaign in a climate dominated by controversy over the increasingly discredited back to basics policy.

The state should be kept out of our personal lives... everybody is entitled to his or her privacy. What my neighbours get up to in private is their business not mine. It is not for the state to interfere.
Edwina Currie, House of Commons, 21 February 1994

But this was not the work of Edwina Currie alone. The introduction of the Bill was the culmination of a carefully planned lobby involving many lesbian and gay activists over a period of 18 months. TORCHE played its part by organising a deluge of mail to make Tory MPs conscious of the strength of the pink vote. Parliamentary support also came from Labour leader John Smith, Neil Kinnock, Mo Mowlam and Liberal Democrat leader Paddy Ashdown, as well as Conservative MPs Harold Elletson and Jerry Hayes, who put their names to the relevant amendment to the Criminal Justice Bill. It was clearly the lack of support from Conservative MPs which caused the motion for an equal age of consent (at 16) to fail and a reduction to 18 to succeed (which many view as no success at all). Only 42 Conservative MPs voted for 16, while 112 (including John Major) voted for 18, many expressing a homophobic desire to protect young gay men from older 'predatory' homosexuals. Alarmingly, 134 Tory MPs voted for the age of consent for gay male sex to remain at 21.

We need to protect young men from activities which their lack of maturity might cause them to regret. Those arguments are the key considerations in this debate. Michael Howard, Home Secretary, House of Commons, 21 February 1994

The lesbian and gay communities are divided over the question of whether recent developments within the Conservative Party are to be welcomed or regarded with mistrust. Many question the fact that there can be sincere support for lesbians and gays among a majority of Tory MPs; others think that we should capitalise on whatever support we can get.

Any gay man or lesbian persuaded to support the Conservatives in return for this sort of concession was duped. And it's time that Sir Ian acknowledged publicly that he was duped too. 'Pink Paper', 11 April 1993

My view is that lesbians and gays should fight for our rights on whatever front is the best one for us to fight on. Lisa Power

When I'm feeling generous politically, I hold the view that there are many locations of struggle. It's the Left that insists that there is only one location of struggle – this strike, this industrial dispute is the one thing we must put our energy into. Linda Bellos

Although I am deeply sceptical about how many of the reforms suggested by TORCHE will be pursued by a Conservative government, I do believe that the Tory position on lesbian and gay rights is less problematic than many people on the Left make out. The range of reforms TORCHE proposes shows that Tories can go pretty far in fighting for lesbian and gay equality (if not as far as Labour Party policy, which offers job protection and lesbian and gay rights at local government level). But we also need to take into consideration the lack of emphasis Conservatives place on civil rights in general. Conservative campaigns prioritise the free market, law and order and a return to traditional family values rather than the creation of a more equal society. And lesbian and gay equality, along with other civil rights campaigns, is very much a side issue. For many of us, the way our sexual identity is viewed is a central concern. So those of us who see the need for lesbian and gay equality as a dominant factor in our lives – along with those of us who link this struggle to the fight for a more equal society for everyone – will vote for the party most likely to bring that about.

If I was a rich gay man it would be totally rational for me to be a Tory, to say, 'well, I'm gay but I have enough money to make it reasonably comfortable so I've decided low income tax and all the things that come with a Tory government are more important to me. Rebecca Flemming, Labour Campaign for Lesbian and Gay Rights (LCLGR)

Everyone I have spoken to has always admitted that they are voting Tory not because the Conservatives are right, but because of their pockets. Brian Stone, DELGA

Sexuality is only one of a number of factors that are important. If you are saying to me as a whole person, does the Labour Party or left-wing politics have any relevance to your life, the answer is, 'Yes, because they threaten it enormously'. Paul Barnes, TORCHE

Gay Tories' objectives stop at limited legal reform. They do not want to transform society. But for many people, myself included, legal reform is only a step on the road to equality; other more fundamental changes are necessary to produce a society in which we all have equal citizenship. The fight for lesbian and gay equality is inseparable from wider issues of social justice: from challenging the way society is structured in terms of class and privilege, racial inequality, gender roles, and notions of 'sexual normality' and 'family'. Lesbian and gay Conservatives want to slot us more equitably into the existing social order, whereas some of us believe that the existing social order is part of the problem.

Gay Conservatives don't want change. They merely want to be tolerated. They want to be able to buy into everything that is shitty about this country. Linda Bellos

You can be gay and Tory, but I imagine it must be impossible to be 'queer' and Tory. Tories have personal investment in maintaining the status quo, while queers aim to demolish it. Cherry Smyth

I think it depends what we mean by 'lesbian'. If we are reducing the argument to sexual orientation, it is possible to be fascist and lesbian, but if we are talking about lesbian feminism in which we try to project an alternative way of loving, an alternative way of relating to each other, then I don't think Conservatism is compatible with lesbian politics or lesbian liberation. Teresa Hope

The Liberal Democrat position

Liberal: favouring individual liberty, free trade, and moderate political and social reform. 'Concise Oxford Dictionary'

Liberal Democrats last week adopted the most radical and comprehensive lesbian and gay rights policy yet seen in mainstream politics.
'Pink Paper', September 1989

The liberal tradition dates back to the philosophical writings of John Locke (1632–1704), Tom Paine (1737–1809), Jeremy Bentham (1784–1832) and J. S. Mill (1773–1836). Essentially, liberals believe that individuals should be free to do as they please, provided they do not infringe the liberty of anyone else. Liberal principles have been used to guarantee the rights of individuals, to argue for redistribution of wealth and power and to limit state intervention. Mill, who co-authored many polemical political treatises with his wife, Harriet Taylor, was a champion of the working classes and of women's rights.

Between the late 1860s and the First World War, the Liberal Party was one of the two major parties in Britain, though since the foundation of the Labour Party in 1900 liberal politics have been in decline. Nevertheless, the continued existence of a liberal party in the shape of the Liberal Democrats (formed on 3 March 1988 from the merger of the Liberal and Social Democratic parties and led by Paddy Ashdown) is proof that the liberal tradition lives on. Indeed, modern liberalism retains much of its original character and its preoccupation with individual liberty.

Liberal Democrats put people first. We aim to create a society in which all men and women can realise their full potential and shape their own success.
'Liberal Democrat Manifesto', 1992

Liberals have often been supporters of lesbian and gay rights; Bentham himself wrote positively about homosexuality. Liberal principles lend themselves well to fighting for lesbian and gay equality, not in the name of 'social justice' but on the grounds that most forms of consensual sexual expression do not interfere with anyone else. Also, according to liberal philosophy, diversity – including sexual diversity – is a positive thing which enriches our society.

Politics is about removing the barriers to self-growth – that's essentially the Liberal Democratic position. Brian Stone, DELGA

Formal support for lesbian and gay rights within the Liberal Party came in 1974 with a commitment to an equal age of consent for gay male sex. Then in 1975 Liberal MP Clement Freud tried to set up a Parliamentary Group to liaise with lesbian and gay groups about law reform. The first major statement on lesbian and gay rights by any political party in Britain was made by the Liberal Party in 1979. To accompany this, a 'special' manifesto called 'The Rights of Gay Men and Women' was published which called for legal equality, laws to outlaw anti-gay discrimination, a Bill of Rights and an Anti-Discrimination Board. The 1987 Alliance Manifesto committed a Liberal/SDP government to introducing a Bill of Rights to protect the civil rights of citizens regardless of their sexual orientation; proposed anti-discrimination employment laws; and contained a promise to equip the NHS to deal effectively with the AIDS epidemic. But Liberal support, as with support from the Labour Party, has wavered. Liberal spokesman Simon Hughes initially expressed support for Clause 28 on the grounds that lesbians and gays should not be given 'special privileges'. As with the Labour Party, this support was subsequently retracted and a motion was passed at the Social and Liberal Democrats' conference in November 1988 which committed the party to repealing Section 28 and to fighting for lesbian and gay equality.

Democrats for Lesbian and Gay Action (DELGA) was formed on 12 June 1988 and is now officially recognised by the party and consulted regularly on matters of policy (this is not the case with any of the other lesbian and gay groups with political affiliations). Finally, the 1992 Liberal Democrat Manifesto contains a comprehensive and uncompromising commitment.

A forward-looking society places equal value on the contribution of all of its citizens – and benefits from the participation of all. Yet in today's Britain many groups of individuals are systematically discriminated against by a society which fails to recognise their right to equality of opportunity. Liberal Democrats will:-
Fight discrimination by incorporating the European Convention on Human Rights into UK law and then extending it into a full Bill of Rights. This will reinforce existing protection in British courts against discrimination on the grounds of sex, race, age, disability, religion or sexual orientation. We will set up a Commission of Human Rights to assist individuals to take legal action in cases of discrimination or other breaches of the rights guaranteed in the Convention.
Guarantee equal rights for gay men and lesbians through changes to criminal law, anti-discrimination legislation and police practices. We will repeal Section 28 of the 1988 Local Government Act. We will create a common age of consent regardless of gender or sexual orientation.
'Liberal Democrat Election Manifesto', 1992

On 21 February 1994 all Liberal Democrat MPs present voted to reduce the age of consent for gay men to 16. But Simon Hughes MP moved an amendment proposing a reduction to 17 on the grounds that 'We should seek to make sure that young people are not victims of significantly older people who could look to them, not for a permanent relationship but simply for their personal gratification.' Such remarks can only call into question the sincerity of Liberal Democratic understanding of lesbian and gay equality.

On paper, the Liberal Democrats are ahead of the other parties. But might the philosophy of 'tolerance' rather than social justice limit them?

We are fighting for lesbian and gay liberation and we make a distinction between that and rights. Rights are something you get along the way to liberation – they are not the end result. I think the liberal conception is based on ideas of tolerance and stops with rights. But at some point you have to ask why lesbians and gay men are discriminated against, why there is prejudice? The liberal notion of, 'Well, there are a lot of people who are prejudiced' doesn't ring true to me. It doesn't explain historical trends and dynamics, the way sexuality is organised and viewed by individuals and by the Church and state. Rebecca Flemming, LCLGR

I find Liberal Democrats more insidious than the Conservative Party because they have the face of tolerance. At least with the Tories you know where you stand. Teresa Hope

Applying liberal principles to real problems undoubtedly has its pitfalls. For instance, in 1956 the Wolfenden Committee drew a distinction between public and private behaviour on the basis of liberal reasoning. Members of the committee thought that it was acceptable for men to commit consensual homosexual acts in private, but drew the line at giving expressions of homosexuality in public the same status as expressions of heterosexuality. This is not a recognition of homosexual equality, but rather a concession that we will not be persecuted as long as we keep out of sight.

Looking at the proposals of the Liberal Democrats, however, it does appear that something more than tolerance is on offer. Government intervention to guarantee individual liberty is implied in many of the propositions, for instance the setting up of an Anti-Discrimination Board and introduction of anti-discrimination laws. But the underlying motivation is still to guarantee individual liberty, a concept which implies a limited understanding of inequality and the nature of discrimination. Ultimately, liberal philosophy is based on the idea that we should all tolerate each other's different beliefs and behaviours (up to a point) and gives little indication of where to draw the line or how and why discrimination exists. In the end, moral judgments have to be made, and my own include the idea that homophobia is wrong on the grounds that it is unjust arbitrarily to brand a whole section of society as inferior. That is a different notion altogether from support for individual liberty, tolerance or cultural diversity.

Strength in autonomy?

❛ The core of contemporary politics has changed: it is increasingly about the individual and self-organisation rather than simply the individual and the state. ❜
Martin Jacques, 'Sunday Times', 18 July 1993

❛ If you think there will always be homophobia, there will always be sexism, there will always be racism, then your strategy is completely different: you stop trying to convince other people to like you and your effort is based instead on building political power for your constituency. That's where I am right now. ❜
Sarah Schulman

It isn't only the political parties that determine the modern political scene. Autonomous pressure groups, mass movements and individual activists play an important role – whether the issue is racism, feminism, the environment or the arms race. Like political parties, pressure groups are organisations that seek to bring about political change. But unlike parties, pressure groups usually focus on a specific issue and do not have policies that cover other areas. They do not aim to become part of government but seek instead to influence public opinion and government through campaigning, lobbying and publicising their cause. CND, Greenpeace, and Feminists Against Censorship are all examples of this type of political intervention.

Autonomous pressure groups are not a new phenomenon. The nineteenth century saw a proliferation of such groups to campaign for the abolition of the slave trade, votes for women and the working classes and so on. Since the 1960s, however, there has been a considerable rise in the numbers and membership of pressure groups, while party membership has declined (the Labour Party now has only 200,000 members compared with a million in the early 1950s). The major beneficiaries of this trend away from party politics have been the causes of feminism, anti-apartheid, civil liberties, anti-racism, nuclear disarmament and environmentalism. Perhaps even lesbian and gay politics.

Explanations for this phenomenon abound. Some see it as a consequence of the emphasis on the power of the individual fostered during the Thatcher years; others as a result of higher educational standards which have encouraged independent thinking. Other explanations include the more diverse needs found in a multi-cultural society, the decline in automatic class-determined political allegiances, the sense of powerlessness generated by the intensification of the arms race, and a crisis in traditional party politics. But whatever the reasons, the result is that our political culture has diversified and new political spaces have opened up. If we wish to be politically active, there is now a multitude of different groups in which to put our energy.

Within the arena of lesbian and gay politics, at the time of writing, the major autonomous pressure groups are OutRage, a radical direct action against homophobia group, and Stonewall, a lobbying group which uses professionals, experienced campaigners and volunteers to campaign primarily for law reform. Is this a misguided way of organising – a retreat to self-interest and individualism? Is it simply our only option after four successive terms of Tory rule? Or does it represent the most powerful form of political expression open to us?

Autonomous organising in the past

There is a strong history of campaigning through autonomous pressure groups in both the lesbian and gay and women's movements. Within lesbian and gay politics the tradition goes back to the Homosexual Law Reform Society (HLRS) formed in May 1958 in the wake of the Wolfenden Report to campaign for the implementation of the report's recommendations and to provide emotional support and counselling for gay men. On 7 October 1964 Labour councillor Allan Horsfall helped found the North Western Homosexual Law Reform Committee, affiliated to HLRS. This group achieved a high profile with a membership of 6,000 at its peak, including a small number of women. In 1969 it became the Campaign for Homosexual Equality (CHE), which still exists. In addition to campaigning work, CHE provided emotional support (Friend, a nationwide support group for lesbians and gay men started out as its counselling arm) and strove to establish an alternative social network to the commercial scene. The general style of CHE, like HLRS, is moderate (some would say apologetic) and it deliberately eschews party politics in order to represent a wide range of people.

The earliest lesbian organisations in Britain were the Minorities Research Group (founded in 1963) and Kenric. Neither was political in any sense – their main function was to provide emotional support. The Minorities Research Group counselled lesbians in a member's flat and then began to organise social gatherings in pubs. In 1965 it abandoned these in favour of setting up a magazine, *Arena Three*. Several members then set up Kenric in order to continue the social function of the group, arranging meetings in homes and once a month at a club. These groups helped many lesbians to overcome their isolation and served to promote a sense of lesbian identity.

The formation of the GLF in November 1970 transformed the shape of lesbian and gay politics. No longer was it enough simply to ask for change;

it was time to demand change.. But GLF's approach was not welcomed by everyone. The organisation's radical politics antagonised many, including some members of CHE who thought GLF's uncompromising approach would be counter-productive.

[GLF's] members, who include both sexes, incline to display a neurotic state of emotionalism which is out of date in the light of recent reforms and creates hostility rather than sympathy even amongst the most liberal minded. The organisation has associated itself with Marxism, although Marx had no homosexual tendencies, and has demanded 'all power to oppressed people'. A great deal of this oppression is now more imaginary than real.
Ian Harvey, member of CHE and ex-Conservative Minister, 'New Statesman', 9 April 1971

The period from the mid-1970s to the late 1980s was relatively quiet as far as autonomous lesbian and gay activism is concerned. GLF had dissolved and many lesbians and gay men joined left-wing groups or took advantage of the growing commercial scene. A number of smaller pressure groups such as Lesbians and Gays Against Nazis, as well as some new professional groups, were formed. CHE remained active, achieving a measure of publicity in 1975 for an Equality Bill it was promoting. And the 1980s saw annual Lesbian Strength marches in London involving hundreds of women.

Much lesbian energy was absorbed in the women's movement. Women's groups and centres were set up across the country and issue-based groups such as Fight the Alton Bill, Campaign Against Pornography, Women Against Pit Closures and various peace initiatives were established. Despite the hostility of some heterosexual feminists, particularly at the outset of the WLM, many lesbians found women's groups more comfortable and relevant to their concerns than lesbian and gay groups, which were often male-oriented and sexist. This was certainly true of CHE, which experienced a lesbian walk-out in 1974.

Activism today

The current wave of lesbian and gay activism was sparked by the outrage that followed Clause 28 and the growing sense of frustration generated by the AIDS crisis. The Organisation for Lesbian and Gay Action (OLGA), set up to co-ordinate the lobby against Clause 28, was the largest of several campaigning groups launched at the time, with over 600 members.

In January 1989, the Aids Coalition to Unleash Power (ACT-UP) was formed in London along the lines of the American group of the same name already well known for its angry and imaginative protests designed to force action to counter the spread of HIV/AIDS. Soon after the group was set up it organised a demonstration against the profits being made out of the anti-HIV drug AZT at the annual shareholders meeting of the drug company Wellcome, floated helium-filled condoms over the walls of Pentonville prison as a protest against the government's refusal to distribute condoms to prisoners and zapped the offices of the *Daily Mail* after journalist George Cale described active homosexuals as 'potential murderers'.

After Clause 28 became law, OLGA formulated a post-Clause agenda which included monitoring the effects of the Clause and fighting for the broader aim of equality. Unfortunately by March 1990 the group was struggling for survival, but out of its ashes rose OutRage, formed on 10 May 1990 and committed to non-violent direct action and civil disobedience. The tactics of the GLF were an inspiration, as were those of the turn-of-the-century suffragettes and contemporary activist groups in the US such as ACT-UP and Queer Nation. It seemed that in Britain in 1990, with Clause 28 law and the AIDS crisis worsening, there was nothing to gain by being reasonable. OutRage tried to mobilise lesbians as well as gay men, in line with the trend in queer politics towards a stronger alliance between the two. At one point OutRage had a lesbian sub-group, LABIA (Lesbians Answer Back in Anger), but this was disbanded in 1992, along with the black caucus, on the grounds that the sub-groups created disunity.

OutRage soon became spectacularly successful at capturing media attention. Hardly a week goes by without a report of an action in the gay press, not to mention some significant mainstream coverage. Kiss-ins, mass weddings, zapping schools with leaflets about safer sex and demonstrations against homophobia from individuals such as pop star Marky Mark and ragga star Shabba Ranks have been among its more creative publicity-generating activities. But in much the same way as the GLF, OutRage has aroused controversy within the lesbian and gay communities. Some feel alienated by its over-the-top stunts (and its largely white male membership) and see a lot of what it does as counter-productive. For some, civil disobedience groups are by their very nature elitist, since it is only certain sectors of the population who are in a position to risk arrest – those who are fully out, without dependents and with sympathetic (or no) employers. And police treatment of middle-class whites is likely to be more lenient than that of blacks. Many see OutRage's strategies as symptomatic of the failings of queer politics in general: at its core appears to be a reverence for style, aesthetics and indulgence at the expense of political vision.

I find it sad that we still have to do things like that. It verges on decadence. It's about plastering our sexuality on walls. Teresa Hope

There were MPs who would have voted for 16 who were put off by this bunch of screamers. Peter Bottomley, Conservative MP for Eltham

The sight of a queen in a nun's habit and a dyke in a strap-on will not bring this racist, bigoted class-ridden society to its knees. Let's stop pretending that it will. Doing something because you get a kick out of it is a good enough reason. Why dress it up as something radical?
Louise Trewavas, 'Rouge', Issue 11, Summer 1992

I like their confrontational tactics – that's what gets change. On the other hand, I think their critique is dubious. It's a bunch of tactics to gain publicity without any real understanding of what it is they're seeking to do. Linda Bellos

The Stonewall Group was set up in May 1989, also in the wake of the Clause 28 campaign, but with a different outlook. Actors Sir Ian McKellen and Michael Cashman and a number of other celebrities who had been involved with the Clause 28 Arts Lobby joined up with journalist Duncan Campbell, former Conservative MP Matthew Parris and various lesbian and gay rights campaigners including Lisa Power to establish a professional campaigning and lobbying organisation along the lines of HLRS and CHE. They rejected the idea of a mass membership and decided to keep decision-making in the hands of a small committee.

Lesbians have a relatively high profile within the group, particularly since the appointment of Angela Mason as Executive Director in 1992. But Stonewall has been criticised for its elitist structure and for representing the lesbian and gay communities to politicians such as John Major without any mandate. In addition, many people feel that to campaign patiently for legal reform is inappropriate; it degrades us to go begging for what should be our rights. Others see Stonewall as bringing a much-needed professionalism and respectability to lesbian and gay politics.

I think the Stonewall Group shows in a nutshell what is wrong with the bourgeois way of organising. I'm not saying that I wish the Stonewall Group was struck by lightning, but I'm very critical about the sort of aspirations they have. For example, say the age of consent was reduced to 16, what would that mean in reality? Very little in my view. It would be a victory and it would give people confidence but in terms of cops picking up guys off the street or raiding cottages it wouldn't make a bit of difference. Kate Richardson, Socialist Workers Party (SWP)

The Stonewall versus OutRage debate boils down to an argument over whether assimilationist or radical approaches to political activism are more effective, a debate that plagued the suffragette campaigns and many other lobbying movements. Assimilationists favour moderate strategies and ask for modest reforms, stressing that lesbians and gay men are 'normal' people who only want the same rights as anybody else. Gay people are presented as respectable members of society in a position to talk to those in power on equal terms. More radical organisations use dramatic methods to draw attention to homophobia in the belief that shock tactics will increase the chances of getting the message across. And even if no change is forthcoming, the nature of the demonstration highlights the strength of feeling and gains publicity. Some would say this polarity is advantageous: there is nothing to prevent you from using both approaches.

Assimilationist groups serve a really important function. We need to learn how to use those groups and not trash them. Sarah Schulman

GLF was a highly political movement and there were lots of things going on within it. Stonewall is just an organisation within the movement, it's not a movement in itself and it doesn't try to be one. It tries to articulate the lesbian and gay cause within a sector where people are in a position to make changes. It tries to make a case for those changes. Angela Mason, Stonewall

Stonewall and OutRage are often described as acting in concert, in that OutRage's dramatically staged demands make Stonewall's more low-key requests seem highly reasonable. Certainly in the 1990s the lesbian and gay movement is no longer a few men sending letters and making phone calls from somebody's front room, but a highly sophisticated enterprise engaging with the media, parliament and the general public. How can that be anything but a good thing?

Mixed reactions

Pressure politics is not without its critics. Many feel that autonomous pressure groups are too narrowly focused and that the issues they address cannot be tackled in isolation, but are part of more wide-reaching political reform. According to this analysis, pressure groups are an inefficient use of energy that could be placed productively in a unified movement or party. The history of such groups shows a destructive tendency to sectarianism and a high turnover of recruits, meaning that new members or organisations are in danger of having constantly to reinvent the wheel. Another worry is fragmentation: the fact that instead of a unified 'lesbian and gay movement' with agreed aims and strategies, there is only a series of uncoordinated groups, none of which seems to last very long. Others would argue that pressure groups such as CND or the Women's Peace Movement have achieved spectacular successes. Moreover, such groups are a means of empowering those individuals who join them.

Fragmentation and not a lot of communication between groups means things are duplicated and things fall down the middle. Rebecca Flemming, Labour Campaign for Lesbian and Gay Rights (LCLGR)

The failure to win the vote for equality on the age of consent shows that tea and biscuits with the Tories is not enough. Neither are publicity stunts. We need organisation and mass action – we need to force the Labour and trades union movements into action alongside us to beat back the homophobic atmosphere created by the Tories, the victimisations at work, the anti-gay laws and discriminatory council policies. Helen Redwood, Militant Labour

The idea of a movement implies a unified voice. I'm keen on diversity. Brian Stone, Liberal Democrats for Lesbian and Gay Action (DELGA)

I don't think organisations should last very long. I think a couple of years is OK because it is not organisations that make change, it is the creative counter-culture that demands change. A lot of people have been affected by ACT-UP even if they never joined it. They've been a lot more out and more aggressive, more demanding, more angry. Sarah Schulman

For some, lesbian and gay-identified pressure groups, however outrageous, are simply not radical enough and will never succeed unless issues of class, race and gender enter the equation. Homocult, a highly controversial Manchester-based group, produces satirical propaganda designed to get class politics back into the lesbian and gay movement, which it has characterised as 'just sipping wine and chatting over gay rights'. It has produced a provocative book called *Queer with Class*, posters and other works of 'cultural terrorism'. One of its most infamous interventions unleashed a wave of fury in the run-up to Europride 1992. A poster, placed in *Capital Gay*, depicted a grinning girl with plaited hair rattling a collecting tin with a swastika on it. The Europride logo was placed at the bottom, the object being to draw attention to the fascist connotations of the word 'Euro'. Homocult has certainly highlighted some of the problems of complacency and elitism – and of working without an overall ideology – inherent within autonomous lesbian and gay politics.

The middle-class leaders of the lesbian and gay ghetto need to perpetuate the idea that homosexuality is a good reason for standing together. It is in their interest to inflict tight controls on this self-created ghetto. They play on the fear of those of us who are exploring our feelings outside the state-defined norm, by making out that they have all the answers, all the culture we need, that our backgrounds and families have failed us, therefore we are classless and easy prey for their bland indoctrination of lesbian and gay identity. Homocult, 'Rouge', Issue 12, Summer 1992

There is this notion that we all have something in common because we are gay. I don't agree with that because I think class always comes into it. In fact, divisions that exist in lesbian and gay groups are to do with class. Kate Richardson, SWP

The fact that it's mainly white middle-class men who get involved in lesbian and gay pressure groups is very obvious. How many black people go to the Stonewall Ball, for example? Teresa Hope

Many lesbians feel excluded from lesbian and gay politics on the grounds that groups are dominated by white middle-class gay men and suffer from sexism and racism, however good their intentions. This is reflected in the priorities and agendas of such groups: equalising the age of consent, issues around HIV/AIDS, protecting cottages and preventing queer-bashings (meaning attacks on gay men rather than lesbians). It is also reflected in their membership and organisation: it's a brave woman who challenges a room of 50 men with only a handful of other dykes in evidence. It's a problem that has come and gone over the past 30 years, begging the question as to whether mixed groups will ever be satisfactory vehicles for lesbian politics.

I get a feeling that it is not that there are too many pressure groups, but that there are too many pressure groups for gay men. Megan Radclyffe

I wouldn't work in a mixed group on gay issues. I feel the power relation blurs me and heterosexual women into the same. Katrina Howse

But rather than forming our own pressure groups, it seems that we have focused our energies elsewhere, such as in the women's, Labour and trades union movements, in providing practical support through social groups and helplines, creating an alternative lesbian culture and organising on the commercial scene. Is it different priorities, political apathy, discontent with existing ways of organising, burn-out or something else?

I think some lesbians are quite contented because if there's nothing in the law books against us, why should we bother? Megan Radclyffe

At a recent meeting where a lesbian pressure group was proposed, the lesbians present said that they were just as disillusioned with other lesbians as they were angry with gay men and straight society. Cherry Smyth

Recent attempts to set up lesbian pressure groups in Britain have met with little success; indeed LABIA, the disbanded OutRage sub-group, was the only one anyone could name. In the US, by contrast, the Lesbian Avengers, founded in June 1993, has mobilised large numbers of women. It defines itself as a 'direct action group focused on issues vital to lesbian survival and visibility'.

Lesbian Avengers is not about trying to win any of the issues. It is about getting lesbians to have good experiences participating in political rebellion and learning how to organise. Sarah Schulman

One recent action in New York under the banner of 'Lesbians Lust for Power' involved rolling a large bed covered with 'undulating lustful activist lesbians' down Broadway. Other innovative stunts have included marching down Fifth Avenue during rush hour with flaming torches, 'Lesbians Go Shopping' visibility actions and handing out lollipops labelled 'Lesbians Taste Good! Lick Homophobia!' The Avengers have developed a style which is sexy, subversive, witty and highly visual. Steps have been taken to set up a Lesbian Avengers Chapter in London, but given current divisions, apathy and general depoliticisation, it remains to be seen whether such a group will succeed.

What relevance is Left?

> *Pulling together 100,000 people for EuroPride is amazingly what we've reached. No other reforming movement can do that now. It's the guilty secret of the Left, for example, that we are the real radicals.* 'Pink Paper', 13 September 1992

The fight for lesbian and gay equality has come a long way since the late nineteenth century. People no longer titter with embarrassment at the mere mention of homosexuality and many view us as a group with legitimate rights. Lesbians, 25 years ago the backroom girls of both the feminist and the lesbian and gay movements, have a higher profile and more political and social recognition than ever. Here are some of the positive signs:

- in 1990 the first lesbian and gay television series, *Out on Tuesday*, was broadcast on Channel 4. Lesbian Caroline Spry was its commissioning editor
- in 1992 the first STD clinic specifically for lesbians, the Bernhard clinic, was opened at Charing Cross Hospital in London
- in May 1993 Amnesty International adopted its first gay prisoners of conscience
- in October 1993 two Scottish lesbians sacked for their sexual orientation won an out-of-court settlement in a case alleging sex discrimination
- in November 1993 the BBC issued guidelines banning the stereotyping of lesbians and gays
- in 1993 and 1994 innovative lesbian characters appeared in Channel 4's *Brookside*, the comedy series *Roseanne* and BBC programmes *Rides* and *EastEnders*
- in May 1994 the Lord Chancellor announced that sexual orientation will no longer be taken into account when appointing judges
- in June 1994 a lesbian co-parent was awarded joint custody of a child with the biological mother
- by mid-1994 there were eight glossy lesbian and/or gay magazines available nationally.

So who or what has had the most influence in securing what gains we have made: liberalism, the activities of lesbian and gay pressure groups, the Labour Party, the New Left (feminists included) or even the Tories?

The most significant advances have been from the socialist end in the sense that the GLC did brilliant things for lesbian and gay rights. But as a whole nothing of significance has happened as a result of the Labour Party. In fact, the most significant changes post 1967 have been made by the Tories.
Brian Stone, Liberal Democrats for Lesbian and Gay Action (DELGA)

The reliance of the women's movement and the lesbian and gay movement on local government secured minimal advances on controlled state power and minimal state resources and was generally demobilising; it didn't create a sound base for those movements. Elizabeth Wilson

The Left is much more inclined to support a schedule of rights which embraces diverse identities than the Right is; the Right doesn't like the language of rights except when we are talking about consumer charters, the rights of citizens to consume. Bea Campbell

I don't think lesbian and gay issues are specifically left-wing issues. But I do think that there is an affinity which needs to be worked on. It's quite clear to me that if you are a lesbian who has been given a hard time for your sexuality you will relate better to other people who have been picked on for other reasons. So there should be a better understanding of issues of social justice, not letting people just sink or swim, because most lesbians and gays have also felt the need for support, for a community. And in a way that's what left-wing politics is about – working for a community, improving everybody's lot.
Lisa Power

From the late 1980s lesbian political energy and debate has increasingly been channelled through popular culture – whether magazines, books, television programmes, theatre, comedy acts, music, photography or film. An ever-growing number of fringe and mainstream artists such as kd lang, Jeanette Winterson, Della Grace, Joan Nestle, Sarah Schulman, Pat Parker, Lee Delaria and Jewelle Gomez, television programmes with lesbian characters, newspaper and magazine articles, and out celebrities such as Pam St Clements and Martina Navratilova are helping to shape lesbian identity and to gain us acceptance and visibility. A stronger cultural presence can give us a greater sense of self-worth, a better understanding of our history and our lives, and may enable younger lesbians to come out with less heartache. It can also change public opinion and attitudes. Even lesbian chic has brought some political advantage: in future, we will not have to battle against the negative stereotype of lesbians as unattractive man-haters in dungarees that made it so difficult for us to be taken seriously in the past. Perhaps no engagement with wider political debates is necessary?

In my view, whatever progress is made in the area of lesbian cultural representation, there must also be real change in societal attitudes and legal and constitutional reform if we are to achieve equality. It is therefore essential to engage politically at parliamentary level and to see the fight for lesbian and gay equality as part of other struggles for social justice. In 1994 we may be able to read lesbian books, watch lesbian films, see lesbians in soap operas or on the cover of *Vanity Fair*, but so long as we are treated inequitably before the law and risk ridicule, verbal or physical abuse or loss of employment if we are open about our sexuality, then we have a fight on our hands. Let's not pretend that changes in the mass media mirror the reality of most of our lives.

Asserting our presence is only one stage in a long battle towards a more equal society. My concern is that while we are winning in the visibility stakes, there are other injustices to be tackled, but there is no popular forum in which to do this. Cherry Smyth

What exactly is 'cultural activism'? Has it replaced 'political activism'? If political activists want to change society, do cultural activists want to change the time that Neighbours is broadcast?
Louise Trewavas, 'Rouge', Issue 11, Summer 1992

A pluralistic future

The experience of lobbying in the USA and in Europe proves that talking to politicians of all parties can educate them on lesbian and gay issues and persuade them to act positively.
Sir Ian McKellen, 'Pink Paper', 25 April 1993

Today sexual politics has a home within all major contemporary British political philosophies. Conservatism, liberalism and the Left all claim to have something to offer. Sexuality cuts across the political spectrum – it's more a question of whether you view lesbian and gay equality as a matter of social justice, individual freedom of expression or a question of civil or human rights.

Most people I interviewed for *Lesbians Talk Left Politics*, whatever their political allegiances, were in favour of a pluralistic approach to lesbian and gay politics that embraces autonomous pressure groups, cultural initiatives and groups and individuals working within the major political parties.

I think the lesbian and gay movement has to be diverse. It is vital that it engages with the Right as well as with the Left, not only because there are groups on the Right who have the right to be protected but also because it is the obvious strategic thing to do. Bea Campbell

I don't think lesbian and gay rights should be enshrined in any one section.
Brian Stone, Liberal Democrats for Lesbian and Gay Action (DELGA)

I think all activity is good. I wouldn't go so far as to say that it is equally good, but we can all coexist and do our different things. Rebecca Flemming, Labour Campaign for Lesbian and Gay Rights (LCLGR)

You can't marginalise yourself into far Left politics. You've got to get yourself into the mainstream, which means appealing to the right wing of the Labour Party and the left and right wings of the Conservative Party.
Paul Barnes, Conservative Campaign for Homosexual Equality (TORCHE)

We are a very diverse movement because we are a very diverse group of people. All we have in common is our sexuality and our sense of oppression, and even that isn't particularly shared because it is different for different people. Lisa Power

Perhaps we should look to the US for a model of an effective lesbian and gay movement? There, lesbian and gay politics presents itself as a 'civil rights' movement in much the same way as the black movement. Civil rights embrace human rights, which ensure that every individual is respected and treated fairly, and political rights such as the right to legal equality and the right not to be discriminated against. Civil rights movements can therefore transcend party politics and, most importantly, engage the mainstream.

The American lesbian and gay movement has positioned itself that way quite brilliantly. It was a really good strategic decision. I think that had I been around at the time, I would have opposed it. But actually, it's resonated with people emotionally. Sarah Schulman

I'm not 'ultra Left' – lesbian and gay liberation or nothing. I'm interested in adopting legislation that might make things better. The way you achieve that, I think, is by being the largest possible movement, as broad as possible within clear demands. And by and large, those are civil rights movements.
Rebecca Flemming, LCLGR

But can the civil rights label stick in Britain, given the differences in our political culture? We have no written constitution or Bill of Rights other than the European Convention on Human Rights, which is not incorporated into UK law. And civil rights are difficult to define and enforce. Do they include guaranteeing minimum wages or educational standards? How do you ensure that theoretical rights become a reality? Should it be the English judiciary which protects them?

For me, the struggle for lesbian and gay equality is an indissoluble part of a wider fight for social justice. This does not mean to say that the Left has the monopoly on sexual politics, but rather that the motives that underlie Liberal and Conservative desire for reform do not reflect my own view of what lesbian and gay equality is about. What's at stake for me is a political principle with a moral foundation: that human beings should be treated as equals and should not be discriminated against on grounds of race, class, gender, disability or sexuality. In real terms, this translates into ensuring that individuals have equal rights to life, equal access to education, equal rights at work, and into providing legal protection to prevent these rights from being transgressed. Social justice relates to culture, social practices, structures and beliefs. This is something the Right has never concerned itself with.

Although there are differences between Liberalism and Conservatism, certain values are shared: the importance placed on individual integrity and the desire to limit state power. I would strongly argue that notions of individual liberty are meaningless in a society where equality is not guaranteed through positive steps. For example, in theory women are free to become politicians, university professors or journalists, yet only 9 per cent of MPs, 3 per cent of university professors and 22 per cent of the staff employed in magazines and newspapers are female. It isn't enough to remove the legal barriers which work against equality and then rely on people's individual efforts. Why shouldn't the state play a positive role in creating a more just society?

An engagement with sexual politics may cut across the political spectrum, but not with the same ease or results. The New Left, feminists and the trades union movement all tackle the more complex expressions of heterosexism – in the workplace, in the community, in education, in cultural representation and in human psychology – that other political parties and philosophies neglect or ignore.

The future of Left politics

No one thought Eastern Europe was an ideal socialist state, yet when it collapsed it was as if it had been. It's as though there's been a failure of nerve. Elizabeth Wilson

The traditional Left has a lot to learn from AIDS-awareness campaigns and direct action groups such as ACT-UP and OutRage, who have recognised how to beat the media at its own game. Cherry Smyth

A realistic assessment of what is happening now and optimism about the possibilities of change are very important. I think what has been lost is any recognition of the possibility of change. Rebecca Flemming, LCLGR

There is no escaping the fact that the Left is not the mobilising force it used to be. I believe, however, that the so-called crisis can be ridden out provided the Left can get its act together. The desire for a more just society where the worst excesses of the free market are curbed and where every individual is equally valued and has equal access of opportunity is still present, whether you call it socialism or not. But in order for this desire for justice to amount to anything, changes must be made. These are a few I'd like to see:
- the development of a form of humanistic socialism based on ethical values
- the Labour movement fully to take on board race, gender and

sexuality as issues of social justice and to push these issues towards the top of its political agenda
- a better understanding among more traditional left-wingers of non-parliamentary ways of organising. Strikes, conferences, rallies and demonstrations are valuable, but so too are media campaigns, innovative publicity stunts and cultural ventures
- a rejection of the Radical feminist notion that the parties and institutions of the Left are founded on masculine interests and cannot be changed. The recent Labour Party resolution that women must represent the party in 50 per cent of its target seats at the next general election constitutes a real opportunity for women, including lesbians, to seize more parliamentary power
- the development of a more inclusive, accessible form of feminism. Those of us who wish to fight for women's equality need a more dynamic and powerful way of expressing ourselves
- less scepticism among left-wingers, including feminists, about the value of parliamentary politics and legal and constitutional reforms.

The biggest problems facing the Left today are deep-seated pessimism and a reluctance to look for new solutions. We have to face up to the fact that the Marxist-influenced brand of socialism that gained ground among left-wing activists in the 1960s and 1970s has failed. But a reassessment of what socialism and feminism are about could secure important gains, particularly given the current disarray within the Tory Party and the real possibility that the 1997 general election will return a Labour government to power. The time is ripe for the beginning of a brighter future, the end of cynicism and the chance for Left politics to grow again. That can only be a good thing for the fight for lesbian and gay equality.

Further reading

Lesbian and gay politics

Cant, Bob and Hemmings, Susan, eds, *Radical Records (Thirty Years of Lesbian and Gay History)*, Routledge, 1988

Cooper, Davina, *Sexing the City: Lesbian and Gay Politics within the Activist State*, River Oram Press, 1994

Cruickshank, Margaret, *The Lesbian and Gay Liberation Movement*, Routledge, 1992

Duberman, Martin, Vicinus, Martha and Chauncey Jr, George, eds, *Hidden from History. Reclaiming the Gay and Lesbian Past*, Penguin, 1991

Gay Left, eds, *Homosexuality: Power and Politics*, Allison and Busby, 1983

Gibbs, Liz, ed, *Daring to Dissent: Lesbian Culture from Margin to Mainstream*, Cassell, 1994

Halifax, Noel, *Gay Liberation & the Struggle for Socialism*, SWP, 1988

Jeffrey-Poulter, Stephen, *Peers, Queers and Commons*, Routledge, 1991

Jeffreys, Shiela, *The Lesbian Heresy*, The Women's Press, 1994

Kaufman, Tara, ed, *High Risk Lives (Lesbian and Gay Politics After the Clause)*, Prism Press, 1991

Kitzinger, Celia, *The Social Construction of Lesbianism*, Sage Publications, 1987

Labour Research Department, *Out at Work*, 1992

Lauritsen, John and Thorstad, David, *The Early Homosexual Rights Movement, (1864-1935)*, Times Change Press, 1974

Lesbian and Gay Socialist, Issue 17, Spring 1989, 'The Great Debate: Lesbians, Gays and the Left'

Nestle, Joan, *A Restricted Country: Essays & Short Stories*, Sheba Feminist Publishers, 1987

Queer with Class: The First Book of Homocult, Ms.Ed (The Talking Lesbian) Promotions, 1992

Smyth, Cherry, *Lesbians Talk Queer Notions*, Scarlet Press, 1992

Tatchell, Peter, *Out in Europe*, Channel Four, 1990

Weeks, Jeffrey, *Coming Out*, Quartet Books, 1977

Feminism

De Beauvoir, Simone, *The Second Sex*, Penguin, 1972

Faludi, Susan, *Backlash*, Vintage, 1992

Feminist Review, 'Perverse Politics: Lesbian issues', No. 34, Spring 1990

Feminist Review, 'Sexuality', No. 11, Summer 1982

Firestone, Schulamith, *The Dialectic of Sex: The Case for Feminist Revolution*, Paladin, 1972

Greer, Germaine, *The Female Eunuch*, Paladin, 1971

Harford, Barbara and Hopkins, Sarah, eds, *Greenham Common: Women at the Wire*, The Women's Press, 1984

Kollontai, Alexandra, *Sexual Relations and the Class Struggle*, SWP, 1984

Lovenduski, Joni and Randall, Vicky, *Contemporary Feminist Politics*, Oxford, 1993

M/F No. 7, 'Political Lesbianism and Feminism – Space for a Sexual Politics?' (Hilary Allen)

Millet, Kate, *Sexual Politics*, Virago, 1977

Trouble & Strife, 'When Lesbians Came Out in the Movement' (interview with Sheila Schulman) and 'Greenham Common – So Why Am I Still Ambivalent?' (Ruth Wallsgrove), Issue 1, Winter 1983

Trouble & Strife, 'In Labour' (interview with Sarah Roelofs), Issue 12, Winter 1987

Wilson, Elizabeth and Weir, Angela, *Hidden Agendas: Theory, Politics and Experience in the Women's Movement*, 1986

Wolf, Naomi, *Fire With Fire*, Chatto & Windus, 1993

General politics

Benn, Tony, *Arguments for Socialism*, Penguin 1980

Dworkin, F. E., *Human Rights: Problems, Perspectives and Texts*, Saxon House, 1979

Engels, Frederich, *Origins of the Family, Property and State*, ed Eleanor Burke, Leacock, 1972

Engels, Frederich, *Socialism: Utopian and Scientific*, Foreign Languages Press Peking, 1975

Foote, G., *The Labour Party's Political Thought: A History*, Croom Helm, 1986

Fukuyama, Francis, *The End of History and the Last Man*, Hamish Hamilton, 1992

Hall, Stuart, and Jacques, Martin, eds, *The Politics of Thatcherism*, London 1983

Locke, J., *Two Treatises of Modern Government*, Mentor, 1965

Le Grand, J. and Estrin, S., eds, *Market Socialism*, OUP, 1989

Levitas, Ruth, ed, *The Ideology of the New Right*, Polity, 1986

McLellan, David, *Marxism After Marx*, Papermac, 1980

Miliband, Ralph, *Parliamentary Socialism: A Study in the Politics of Labour*, Merlin, 1960

Mill, J. S., *Utilitarianism, Liberty, Representative Government*, Dent, 1910

Paine, T., *The Rights of Man*, Penguin, 1969

Tatchell, Peter, *The Battle for Bermondsey*, Heretic Books, 1983

Thomson, David, ed, *Political Ideas*, Pelican, 1978

Willetts, David, *Modern Conservatism*, Penguin, 1992

Contacts

ACT UP BM 2995, London WC1N 3XX

Black Lesbian Centre 54-56 Phoenix Road, London NW1 Tel: 071 383 5405

Campaign for Homosexual Equality (CHE) PO Box 342, London WC1X ODU

Campaign Against the Child Support Act PO Box 287, London NW6 5QU
Tel: 071 837 7509

Homocult PO Box 45, Manchester M12 4EA

International Lesbian and Gay Association: UK Group (ILGA)
c/o Nigel Warner, 141 Cloudsley Road, London N1 OEN

Labour Campaign for Lesbian and Gay Rights (LCLGR) PO Box 306,
London N5 2SY

Lesbian and Gay Employment Rights (LAGER) St Margaret's House,
21 Old Ford Road, London E2 9PL Tel: 081 983 0694

Lesbian Information Service PO Box 8, Todmorden, Lancashire OL12 5TZ

Liberal Democrats for Lesbian and Gay Action (DELGA) LD HQ,
4 Cowley Street, London SW1P 3NB

Northern Ireland Gay Rights Association (NIGRA) PO Box 44, Belfast BT1 1SH

OutRage meets Thursdays. Office at 5 Peter Street, London W1
Tel: 071 439 2381 to check venue

Scottish Homosexual Rights Group (SHRG) 58A Broughton Street,
Edinburgh EH1 3SA

Stonewall 2 Greycoat Place, London SW1P 1SB Tel: 071 222 9007

Conservative Campaign for Homosexual Equality (TORCHE) BM/TORCHE,
London WC1X 3XX

Lesbian and gay trades union groups

Association of University Teachers Lesbian and Gay Group c/o AUT,
United House, 1 Pembridge Road, London W11 3HJ

BECTU Lesbian and Gay Network c/o Jane Paul, equality officer, Broadcasting,
Entertainment, Cinematograph and Theatre Union, 111 Wardour Street,
London W1V 4AY

Banking, Insurance and Finance Union Lesbian and Gay Group
25 Ferrara Square, Swansea SA1 1UW

Confederation of Health Service Employees Network c/o Marisa Howes,
Glen House, High Street, Banstead, Surrey SM7 2LH

Civil and Public Services Association Lesbian and Gay Rights Group
c/o Falcon House, Falcon Road, London SW11 2LN

**Institution of Professional Managers and Specialists, Lesbians and Gays in
IPMS** LEGII, PO Box BM 6771, London WC1N 3XX

Lesbian and Gay Trade Union Confederation LGTUC, c/o PO Box BM Rouge, London WC1N 3XX

London Transport Lesbian and Gay Workers' Group PO Box 1965, London N4 2AJ

Manufacturing, Science and Finance, Lesbians and Gays in MSF 64-66 Wandsworth Common North Side, London SW8 2SH

National Association of Probation Officers Lesbian and Gay Group 3-4 Chilvary Road, London SW11 1AT

National Association of Teachers in Further and Higher Education c/o 5 Caledonian Road, London N1 9DX

National Union of Civil and Public Servants Lesbian and Gay Group PO Box BM 1645, London WC1N 3XX

National Union of Teachers c/o LGRWP, 4 Rupert Street, Leicester LE1 5XH

Transport and General Workers' Union Lesbian and Gay Group c/o Transport House, Smith Square, London SW1P 3JB

UNISON, UNISON National Lesbian and Gay Officer 1 Mabledon Place, London WC1H 9AH

Left-wing parties

Militant Labour 3/13 Hepscott Road, London E9 Tel: 081 985 7578

Labour Party 150 Walworth Road, London SE17 1JT Tel: 071 701 1234

Revolutionary Communist Party (RCP) BM, RCP, London WC1N 3XX

Socialist Workers Party (SWP) PO Box 82, London E3 Tel: 071 538 5821

Acronyms and abbreviations

ACT-UP AIDS Coalition to Unleash Power

CHE Campaign for Homosexual Equality

DELGA Liberal Democrats for Lesbian and Gay Action

GLC Greater London Council

GLF Gay Liberation Front

HLRS Homosexual Law Reform Society

ILEA Inner London Education Authority

LCLGR Labour Campaign for Lesbian and Gay Rights

LRC Labour Representation Committee

OLGA Organisation for Lesbian and Gay Action

SWP Socialist Workers Party

TORCHE Conservative Campaign for Homosexual Equality

TUC Trades Union Congress

WLM Women's Liberation Movement